JIM

THE
Spiritual Journey
OF A
VERY ORDINARY MAN

The Search for my
SPIRITUAL ESSENCE

outskirts press

INTRODUCTION

As I have become older, I found that I had a fascination with the things beyond me, such as the religions of the world. I asked, How are they different? How are they the same? Is there a God? If so, how can we prove it? Or is it simply a matter of faith that we believe in God? Why are people spiritual? Does it give them comfort in some way?

Well, these are just a few of the things I want to explore, and I hope you join me on this journey. I may never find answers to the questions I posed above and perhaps many others, but I'm sure I will learn a lot on this journey, and isn't that really the important thing?

When I started on this journey, I wasn't sure where I should start, so I thought, let's first look at the religions of the world. It was as good a place to start as any. As I started to do this studying and writing, I discovered The Great Courses. It is a teaching company that provided a huge number of courses taught by world-renowned college professors and experts in their respective fields. So, I jumped on the bandwagon and ordered courses on religion to start me off. I learned a lot about the major religions of the world, but that was not enough. Just learning about these religions was very interesting, but I felt something lacking. Was I moving in the right direction? Next, I ordered a few courses on philosophy, and that gave me a sense that I was moving in the right direction. Philosophy forced me to look at some tough questions, such as—Is there a God? Do we have free will? Is there a soul? I had to reach deep inside myself to address these truths. Some of these truths I embraced, and yet there were others that I am still thinking about to this day. But the study of philosophy made me realize that I needed to look further to find out the truths of the universe. I needed to study science to learn about what the universe really is, or at least what it is from the point of view of present-day scientists. After taking a number of science courses, I still felt that something was missing. I started to question what reality really was. I needed more, so I took one final course on defining or redefining reality from a scientific point of view. After taking all these courses along with the additional research that I did, I could start to put the pieces together about religion, God, spirituality, the universe, and our reality.

This writing may seem a lot like a "book report" where I report to you what the various professors, experts, and authors have to say on their subject matter. However, be aware that I am not describing the content of each course in detail. I am just pulling out the information that is relevant to what I am trying to present to you. Even though it may seem like a book report, please stick with it, because I will give you my thoughts throughout this work, and in the process of reading it, I think you will form your own opinions. I have provided you with a bibliography at the end for your reference, and I decided not to do footnotes. Instead, I tried to be faithful to the various experts by giving credit to them right up front at the beginning of each of their sections by identifying them and giving you a few details about them, such as what university they are affiliated with and perhaps any awards they received or books they wrote. In writing this work, I have tried to make it as simple as possible for any ordinary man like myself to understand it, but quite frankly, most of the subject matter will require some deep thought. You may even have to reread sections because there is a lot of material that is covered. Also, I tried to have it have a natural flow from beginning to end. Only you can be the judge of whether I succeeded at that endeavor, but I tried to be as clear and concise as I could be with such a wide range of subject matter. If you notice any errors in the facts, it is not the expert's fault. These errors would be mine. Lastly, I looked to Wikipedia and some other websites for some explanations on subject matter that I found was not explained in any of the course material or books that I referenced.

Anyway, if you continue to read the rest of this work, you will follow the arc of my journey. A lot will be informational, but if you stick with it, you will not only see how I learned and evolved but start to think about your place in the universe and start to form your own opinions. I'm not here to force my thoughts and opinions on you in any way. I am hoping that as you read my journey, you will form your own spiritual identity as an end result and that you are satisfied with where you end up at this point in your life.

TABLE OF CONTENTS

Philosophy

Science

Our Reality

Religions

GETTING STARTED
WITH THE RELIGIONS
OF THE AXIAL AGE

I will start my journey with this section on the various early religions of the world. I will cover the religions that emerged during the Axial Age as well as the stage that was set prior to this age which allowed these new ideas to flourish. The Axial Age was from 800 – 200 BCE and was one of the most creative and influential eras in world history. The content of this section is somewhat of a summarization of the information presented in The Great Course called **Religions of the Axial Age: An Approach to the World's Religions** taught by Professor Mark W. Muesse of Rhodes College.

The German philosopher Karl Jaspers termed this epoch die Achsenzeit, or the Axial Age, to indicate the pivotal importance of this age to human thought. At this time moralists, priests, philosophers, and sages grappled with novel ideas about the nature of humanity, the world, and ultimate reality by looking at them with fresh eyes. This era was so important in human history that people today continue to live out their moral and religious lives based on the thoughts and practices developed during this age. The surge of religious and philosophical activity during this age centered in four distinct regions of civilization at the time: East Asia, South Asia, West Asia, and the northeastern Mediterranean. Each of these areas witnessed the emergence of several key individuals whose lives and teachings inspired people to create the traditions that led to the emergence of several religions during this age.

By way of an editorial note for any layman like me, the Axial Age could be thought of as a time when people turned inward for religious and spiritual answers instead of looking at religion solely as a means to provide a good life for man and his family. For example, prior to the Axial age, religion mainly provided rituals for the "here and now" such as rituals to provide for a good growing season, or rituals for fertility for the women of the family, or rituals for safe passage to the next town, etc. During the Axial Age, man was concerned about those things I just mentioned, but he wanted more. He became concerned with his personal destiny. What would happen when he died? Where would he go? Is there really a God or Gods? If so, what would God want him to do? Should he be more morally responsible to others in some way? What is the essence of the reality that we see every day? Should we be as concerned with the character of our soul as with the approaching storm that could destroy the crops in the field? In any event, it was a time of great change and reflection for mankind spiritually.

The Axial Age occurred at a time when there was increasing urbanization and mobility. It was also a time of great political and legal upheaval. This rapid political and social change certainly generated a lot of concern, uncertainty, and insecurity, but interestingly it also provided a time for innovative and creative religious and philosophical thought. It made for a fundamental change in the function of religion in human life. During this era, the purpose of religion shifted from what theologian John Hick called cosmic maintenance to personal transformation. Cosmic maintenance can be considered as religious ritual to keep the world in good working order.

Indo-Iranians or the "Noble Ones"

To begin our journey, we need to go back well over 4,000 years ago to central Asia. There was a people called Indo-Iranians. They called themselves the "Noble Ones." They were a nomadic or semi-nomadic people of animal herders who also hunted wild animals. They were a tribal people with little or no formal governance. They were a peaceful people who had a no nonsense world view who believed in numerous gods. Their gods were practical based on this world view such as the Sun, Moon, Sky, and Earth which controlled their lives. There were ritual practices that were important which included the gods of fire, water, and animal spirits. These were just a few of their many gods that are associated with their various ritual practices. What is important to realize is that these people migrated to many parts of the world over time and brought their culture with them to such places as northern Europe, the northern Mediterranean, Iran, India, and as far west as Ireland. Their single language evolved into many other languages such as Icelandic, German, Gaelic, Latin, Greek, Russian, Persian, Sanskrit, Sinhalese, and English. As you can see these people can well represent our starting point on our Axial Age journey because of their broad influence on the world as it was at that time.

Zoroaster

As the Indo-Iranians drifted south from Central Asia, they came in contact with the Mesopotamians, where they learned to domesticate horses, build war chariots, and fashion weapons which completely disrupted their once stable nomadic or semi-nomadic culture. Many turned to stealing livestock, raiding, and pillaging, which gave many of them a new purpose in life – to gain wealth and glory. This lifestyle disrupted moral concerns and the respect for law and order. Society now had both peaceful people and warriors among the Indo-Iranians.

By the middle of the second millennium BCE, the Indo-Iranians were starting to migrate to their respective areas of the world, as indicated above. We will stay for the moment with the people that migrated to Iran. This is where Zoroaster enters the picture. Little is known of Zoroaster, but we date him around 1200 BCE, just prior to the Axial Age. We believe that he came from a modest semi-nomadic family at a time when cattle rustlers and outlaws were in their prime. It is said that Zoroaster was a priest or an authorized ritual specialist that had a visionary experience. At age thirty, he was led into the presence of the God Ahura Mazda and six other radiant beings called the heptad, "the seven," from which he had a special revelation "to… teach men to seek the right (asha)." He now saw the gods in a moral dimension. Gods were either good or evil. He believed that all humans had to make a choice in life to either be good or be evil and follow their respective gods. The choices that people make would determine their personal destiny. This is certainly a departure from the theology that the gods exist to help in cosmic maintenance only. Zoroaster believed that those choices would not only determine their destiny on earth but also in the afterlife. This was counter to the beliefs of the time that people were here to serve the gods with appropriate sacrifices to make the gods happy. Zoroaster believed that on the fourth day after death, man would be judged and good people would go to heaven to be with the God Mazda and that evil people would go to "hell." He also believed in a final cosmic destiny where at the end of time good would prevail over evil and establish paradise on earth, where there would be a bodily resurrection of the dead, and those living in heaven would return to earth and continue life in physical form. He also believed in a savior figure or an apocalyptic judge, a saoshyant, that would play a big part in determining the overall destiny of humankind.

It is interesting to note that the monotheist religions of Judaism, Christianity, and Islam have a parallel with some of Zoroaster's beliefs. For example, Zoroaster's beliefs in the devil, the Day of Judgment, heaven and hell, angels, and the concept of a divine savior all have parallels with those monotheistic religions. It is a controversial issue, but many scholars believe that perhaps those religions absorbed many beliefs from Zoroaster.

By way of closing out this section on Zoroaster, I want to leave you with a thought that was presented in the course. Is it possible that the wise men who appeared at Jesus' birth were actually Zoroastrians searching for their saoshyant and were led to Judea, where Jesus was born? It is a very interesting thought that possibly sheds a whole new light on the birth of Jesus for Christians.

SOUTH ASIA (INDIA AND PAKISTAN) BEFORE THE AXIAL AGE

We now turn our attention to South Asia, or India and Pakistan. The Indo-Iranians of Central Asia, as you recall, were a nomadic or semi-nomadic people. Some of their descendants, called Indo-Aryans, migrated south to what is now Pakistan. They were pastoral nomads, not agriculturalists. They found a culture already in place in the Indus River Valley, and the meeting of these two cultures ultimately provided for the Hindu family of religions. When the Indo-Aryans arrived around 1500 BCE, the Indus culture was in decline but still potent enough to influence Hinduism. The Indus dwellers were likely peaceful agriculturists that traded with the Mesopotamians, which is now Iraq. For governance, they most likely had a centralized authority with law enforcement. They were deeply concerned with sexuality and procreation, as seen by their artifacts that were uncovered over the ages. They did revere and celebrate the reproductive powers of women, which may account for the Goddess worship of contemporary Hinduism. Indus cities also had sophisticated bathing facilities, suggesting an intense concern with purity and cleanliness above and beyond simple hygiene. Like Hindus today, Indus people were focused on ritual purity not only in bathing but with concerns for food, clothing, and the persons one could associate with and touch. These rituals provided for a sense of order and to cleanse people according to their custom. Additionally, there have been no positively identified sacred buildings of the Indus culture, suggesting that the home served as their sacred place, similar to contemporary Hinduism. There is also no indication that they thought much about the afterlife, thus indicating that their rituals and practices were to provide order in the present.

As mentioned above, by the time the Indo-Aryans arrived, the Indus culture was already in decline. Originally it was thought that the Indo-Aryans conquered the Indus people, but some scholars think that the two cultures were integrated slowly and peacefully. Also, some experts think that the Indo-Aryans were indigenous to the area. Regardless of where they came from, there can be found ancient connections between the Indo-Aryans and the Indo-Iranians.

Our knowledge of the Indo-Aryans comes from the Vedas, which provide instruction, prayers, and hymns created for performing rituals. Today the Vedas are the Hindus' oldest and most sacred scripture of divine knowledge and universal secrets. The Vedas tell us that Indo-Aryan religion principally involved ritual and sacrifice. As in Indus culture, Indo-Aryan ritual appears to focus mainly on acquiring goods for a happy and comfortable existence in the present. The Vedas describe thirty-three different gods that dwell on earth, in heaven, and in the mid-space between the two worlds. The Vedas had little to say about human nature and destiny. The Vedas are more concerned with praising gods and performing rituals than understanding what it means to be human. The Vedas make no pronouncements that human destiny is tied to moral choices, as Zoroaster believed. The Indo-Aryans regarded death as an occasion for grief and sadness, yet there is no indication that death was terrifying or that an afterlife – if there was one – was unpleasant. The Rig Veda, which is the oldest of the Vedas, says nothing of reincarnation, an Axial Age development that received widespread acceptance as the Vedic tradition evolved into Hinduism.

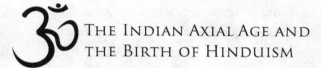

THE INDIAN AXIAL AGE AND THE BIRTH OF HINDUISM

The story of Hinduism is a grand story full of color, variation, and life. It is so different from my upbringing in the Christian faith that I am fascinated by it. Many of the beliefs may sound alien to Christian ears, but one can't deny the appeal and tug Hinduism has on the human heart, so let's start this part of the journey.

As the Indo-Aryans spread and settled over northern India, many started to question the value of the rituals and the power of the priests. Between 800 and 600 BCE, Indian life began to change dramatically. Some Indo-Aryans began to become concerned with their individual fate, and death started to become a matter of serious concern. The Upanishads, a collection of texts later included among the Hindu scriptures, were composed to help find answers to the emerging questions about life, death, and the significance of both.

At the end of the Vedic era and the start of the Axial Age, fears arose that at death one would reach heaven only to find that they could die again. The Vedic era refers to the religious ideas and practices among most Indo-Aryan-speaking peoples of ancient India after about 1500 BCE. These ideas and practices are found in the Vedic texts, and they were one of the major influences that shaped contemporary Hinduism. The word "redeath" entered the religious lexicon, implying that one could reach heaven but die again and dissolve into the elements of the natural world. This was concerning to the people, so out of the concept of redeath eventually a new concept called rebirth was born. Rebirth, or reincarnation, became the fundamental assumption of virtually all Indian religions and philosophies. Though these religions in India at the time interpreted rebirth differently, the common term used to describe it was "**samsara,**" which meant "wandering." To the Indians, rebirth meant that one would be born, die, and be reborn many times over. Rebirth also didn't necessary mean that one would be reborn as a human. One could be reborn as a goat, cow, insect, or whatever. As a note, reincarnation is not unique to India. The belief in reincarnation is found among some Native Americans, also in West Africa, and amongst some ancient Greeks such as Pythagoras and Socrates, just to name a few.

As the Axial Age progresses, the Upanishads develop further details of reincarnation. One of the most important developments is the concept of "**karma.**" Karma came to include moral action. Like Zoroaster's beliefs, the Upanishads make one's moral behavior the decisive element in human destiny and for the Indians their current life and their future lives through rebirth. Karma states that the events of one's life – good or bad – are neither chance occurrences nor foreordained by realities or gods outside of oneself. Rather Karma refers to one's actions and their consequences. Karma does not separate action from consequences. The effects of one's actions will eventually return to the individual in what is known as the "fruiting of karma." Karma is inevitable, always returning to the agent who created it no matter how long it takes, which may span more than one lifetime. Karma pertains not only to physical acts but to one's thoughts and words as well, which points to the growing focus at this time on the spiritual life. Karma can be good or bad, positive or negative. Performing good actions produces good karma. Likewise, wicked or irresponsible actions will produce negative karma. Karma is a principle of absolute justice, a process that occurs impersonally, with no god or divine being meting out justice. According to Hinduism, even the gods are subject to karma.

The ideas of rebirth and karma had a powerful hold on the peoples of India during the Axial Age. Too much bad karma could take one from human existence to that of a buzzard or insect in a future life, for example. Good karma could take someone from a lower Indian caste to that of a higher caste, such as that of Brahmin or priest. The caste system in Indian culture and present-day Hinduism exerts a very strong influence on the people of India. They believe that whatever caste they are born into during a lifetime, that is their station in life. There is no upward movement, so you can see how the people would want to have good karma in the present life if they want to progress to a higher station in a future life. In present-day Hinduism there are several castes or stations in life. This caste system is called Varna. The highest caste is the Brahmins or priests, as already mentioned. The next highest caste is rulers, warriors, and administrators. Then there is the caste of cattle herders, agriculturalists, artisans and merchants. The Shudra caste is formed with the laborers and service providers. These are the four castes in the Varna system in descending order. However, there is a further caste not in the Varna system called Dalits, or the untouchables. The untouchables were the people that performed the lowest functions of human existence such as cleaning latrines, butchering, removal of waste, etc.

Samsara, or rebirth, was not an appealing prospect for most Indians during the Axial Age. The idea of existing in an endless cycle of death and rebirth for all of time was certainly not what most wanted because even in the best of lives there still exists some suffering. Eventually, the concept of moksha appeared. Moksha is the complete liberation from this endless cycle of samsara. As a result, to many people the material things of the world had little meaning, and they believed that to achieve moksha, one should live a homeless and ascetic life of self-discipline and abstinence, and they should pursue a contemplative and spiritual life away from the distractions of the material world. Many of these samanas, as they were called, lived alone in caves or forests. Some wandered from village to village with only a change of clothes and a bowl to beg for food. The relationship between the samanas and ordinary people became symbiotic in Indian culture. The non-ascetics gained good karma by giving the samanas food, clothing, and shelter. Likewise, the samanas were able to help the ordinary people by providing lessons for life and living. This was a very experimental time for these ascetics. How do you achieve moksha? They wandered from place to place seeking gurus for advice, trying different disciplines such as meditation, hatha yoga, self-denial, and even self-mortification to seek the knowledge to achieve moksha.

This knowledge was elusive, but they believed that the pursuit of the deepest principles of reality was their goal in life. The trend to know the world not as a collection of unrelated objects and beings, but as an integrated totality that could be understood by knowing its fundamental basis was so pervasive that this effort is seen as one of the salient characteristics of the Axial Age. The sages searched for the key to basic forces in the cosmos, hoping to reduce them to a singular principle, thus affording genuine freedom and fulfillment and the release from samsara. This knowledge was necessarily extraordinary and could be gained only by rigorous methods of asceticism and introspection, not gained through lectures or read from books. Some ascetics have claimed to have found the way to liberation and the knowledge of the secrets of the universe. Many of these sages recorded their search over the ages in the ancient text called the Upanishads. The general viewpoint of the Upanishads is that the soul is invisible and immortal, never created and never destroyed, and separate from both the body and the mind. These sages believed that to understand ultimate reality which they called Brahman was unattainable. Brahman is said to permeate all things yet cannot be perceived. It embraces good and evil, yet it transcends both. Paradoxically, it encompasses the whole of reality, yet surpasses it. They also believed that everyone had a higher self, called atman. We would think of this atman as our soul, spirit, or mind. Then an epiphany emerged in the later Upanishads. It is said that the concepts of atman and Brahman converge such that the soul is seen as identical to ultimate reality itself, one and the same, and to believe otherwise is the source of our human misery. This "other" belief is called Maya. One can think of Maya as a veil over reality. It deceives us into thinking that we are separate entities when in fact we are not, because atman and Brahman are consubstantial, one and the same.

Well, you can see that the Upanishads give a lot for you to wrap your mind around. The concept that your soul and ultimate reality are one and the same, the Vedantic perspective which is a Hindu philosophy based on the doctrine of the Upanishads, especially in its monistic form , really takes a bit of mental gymnastics. I'm still working to come to some sort of understanding of this concept, but it is very hard to give up the concept of self because quite frankly when I look… there I am… in what appears to be a separate entity called "me."

Anyway, I'm not alone. In the Axial Age, many found the concept too demanding. Ordinary people preferred a spirituality in which ultimate reality could be conceptualized and to which they could relate.

Hinduism then became a family of religions. It embraces differences rather than excluding them. Hinduism recognizes that people may be in different stages in their lives and that the beliefs and practices of one person might not suit another. Most Hindus preferred a more traditional piety focusing on personal gods and goddesses as opposed to the highly abstract Brahman. In the Hindu pantheon there are 330 million gods and goddesses. Wow! Wrap your mind around that for a minute. Anyway, the images of their gods cover the range. They could be humanlike or not. Each Hindu doesn't worship them all, because that would be impractical. Instead each individual usually has a personal deity of choice, ista-devata. Toward the end of the Axial Age, the Bhagavad-Gita was written to help in the personal navigation of the Hindu life. It is the most frequently read Hindu scripture, and it suggests that devotion to God is the best practice of all.

Well, that covers Hinduism in a nutshell. I hope that you have found it as colorful and full of life as I did, but now we move on to the life of Siddhattha Gotama and the start of Buddhism, which appears to have some parallel beliefs to Hinduism, making Buddhism just as colorful and intriguing.

BUDDHISM

Around 490 BCE in south Asia Siddhattha Gotama was born, and it is said that he lived to about the age of eighty. A lot has been said about Siddhattha over the ages. Some stories are historically correct and other stories have been embellished, so as you read about his life here, please take it with a grain of salt. Nevertheless, it is a fascinating story that provided for the birth of a great religion. It is said that he was born into a privileged family. There is some doubt that his family was a royal family, but nevertheless it is said that his father, for most of Siddhattha's life, shielded him from the cruelties of life.

He was raised in an environment that was most pleasant with the best food, best clothes, and the best entertainment. At sixteen, Siddhattha married his cousin, Yashodhara, and they had a son. Life was very good for Siddhattha, but then things changed for him drastically. He went out into the world and encountered three people. One person was very ill. Another person was ravaged by old age. Lastly, he encountered a corpse. He also came upon a wandering samana who had renounced everything but was in a state of happiness. I can almost see his perplexed face as he spoke to the samana and tried to understand how the man could be so happy with so little. Now, at the age of twenty-nine, the realities of life caught up with Siddhattha. Distraught by what he had seen in these four spectacles, which are called the "four sights" by Buddhists, he decided to renounce the life of luxury and take up the life of a samana. Even though Siddhattha was a great man, you still have to question his judgment about abandoning his family and taking up an ascetic life. However, that was the choice he made, and I'm sure that his family was well cared for back home because of their status in life.

Siddhattha, as a novice samana, then started to wander through the cities of the Ganges basin in India in search of ascetics that could teach him the disciplines that could end his samsara. He received guidance from several teachers and practiced meditation but could not find relief from suffering. He then practiced self-mortification, depriving his body of food until he became emaciated. He realized that this practice not only did not end suffering but intensified it. After six years, he then decided that the "middle way" was probably the best approach – not too much excess and not too much deprivation. He then started to take care of his body and started a different type of meditation called "mindfulness." This meditation was different from what he had been taught. While meditating, he paid attention to focusing on his breath, because it brought him a heightened sense of awareness and calm. It made him aware of what was happening in the mind, body, and external environment without judgment. As a result of mindful meditation, Siddhattha believed that the mind would become more receptive to the true nature of the world and the self. While deeply meditating, it is said that a demon tried to tempt him back to the temptations and pleasures of life, however Siddhattha stayed the course and then won the understanding that liberated and conquered samsara. At that point he realized he would never be reborn into this world again. Also, at that point he had earned the title "the Buddha" or the "Awakened One." For forty-nine days the Buddha enjoyed his liberation, and then he decided to go out and teach his insights to others. He talked about his insights and spelled out his "Four Noble Truths," which are considered the essence of Buddhism. The Buddha never expected that his teaching would be accepted on his authority. He wanted people to take responsibility for their convictions. Never accept anything because it is revelation, tradition or from sacred texts. Never accept hearsay or anything because it is logical or rational. Never accept anything because you agree after reflecting on it. Never accept anything because a competent teacher has said to accept it.

The **first Noble Truth** is that life itself is suffering, or "dukkha" from the Pali term. All that we experience – birth, aging, illness, and death – is suffering. Likewise, the presence of displeasing things and the absence of pleasing things is also suffering. Not getting what one wants is also suffering. Changes in our lives and disappointment also cause us to suffer. Suffering is just a fact of life for humans.

Like a true scientist, he then analyzed the human condition with the precision of a surgeon and came up with the **second Noble Truth**. The cause of suffering is desire, which leads to rebirth accompanied by delight and lust. This Nobel Truth is at the heart of the Buddha's vision and separates it from other religious perspectives. Now, the Buddha was not wholly opposed to desire. The problem comes when desire becomes self-centered, with intense cravings for an object which becomes a matter of necessity to possess it. Desire leads to attachment, and both Hinduism and Buddhism recognize this as the continuation of the cycle of rebirth and samsara. If we already possess something and there is a fear of losing it, then this is also desire. Our attachments to things also lead us to resist change. Yet change is at the root of the way the world works. The Buddha believes that change is constant and persistent, and that solid objects are in a state of constant flux. Quantum mechanics seems to confirm the Buddha's view that the foundational elements of the world are more like energy fluctuations than solid, substantial objects or materials. The Buddha believed that the universe or cosmos was a complex array of processes in flux. There will be much more on quantum mechanics later. However, for now, it is not that things change, but that change is the only thing there is. Many people who accept this transience try to slip a sense of permanence in through the "back door." The concept of God is one example. The concept of a soul is another. The Buddha's most distinctive contribution is that there is no permanent, immortal and substantial soul. He believed that there was "no-self," or anatman in Sanskrit (anatta in Pali). He simply believes that thinking about a "self" and a soul are unskillful ways to think about human beings. If you recall in our study of Hinduism, we noted a school of thought that the soul or atman was consubstantial with Brahman or the essence of reality. In other words, they were one and the same. Does that mean that these Hindus believe there was no-self, like the Buddha? I'm not really sure. Do the Hindus mean that self is a part of ultimate reality yet retaining its own identity of self, or do they actually mean that the self as an identity does not exist but is "mixed in" with the rest of reality? The latter, you could say, is more in line with the Buddha's concept of no-self. In any event, it appears that the Buddha had taken a step further in actually declaring that there is no-self.

Rather than viewing individuals as immortal souls housed in a perishable body, he saw humans as an interconnected and ever changing collection of energies or forces which he called the "Five Aggregates of Being."

The first aggregate is matter, which refers to our physical make-up. The second is sensations or feelings. The third is our perceptions of the world. The fourth is mental formations, which are the sources of our desires, cravings, and intention. The fifth is consciousness or our sense of being aware.

Nothing about these components endures, according to the Buddha. Our perceptions, thoughts, bodies, and consciousness are all in a state of flux. There is no permanent subject or agent underlying these "processes." He says that the soul or self is an illusion, in the same way that a rainbow is an optical illusion. We can see the rainbow and all its colors, yet it is not really there to touch. The Buddha says that problems arise when we ascribe reality to this illusion of self. Believing in a permanent, substantial self is the root of suffering, setting in motion a series of thoughts, words, and deeds that precipitate anguish, misery, and disappointment.

The **third Noble Truth** is straightforward. You do not have to suffer. The solution is to stop craving. By stopping the cravings, attachments slip away from us, and we end the cycle of suffering and rebirth. When suffering is ended, we enter into a state of nibbana, or as we in the West call it, nirvana. Like moksha in Hinduism, nirvana can be achieved in life. One who achieves it is called an arahant. At death there is a final nibbana or parinibbana, where all karmic energies sustaining life are dissipated and the arahant is released from the cycle of death and rebirth.

Well, there you have it. Just give up your cravings and you will achieve nirvana. It sounds simple. Right? Not at all, so this is where the **fourth**

Noble Truth helps. Buddha gave his followers a roadmap as the fourth Noble Truth. He developed what is called the "Noble Eightfold Path." It consists of doing the following: have right understanding, right intention, right speech, right action, right livelihood, right effort, right mindfulness, and right concentration. Sounds simple, right? These actions have traditionally been divided into three categories called the "Triple Practice" of study, conduct, and concentration. For our purposes, we can call these practices cultivating wisdom, developing moral conduct, and disciplining the mind. To gain wisdom, one must study and practice the teachings and practices of the way of the Buddha. Developing moral conduct involves not harming any sentient beings such as man or any living creatures (1) and not harming anyone with speech (2), refrain from taking what is not offered (3), refrain from sexual misconduct (4), and refrain from alcohol and substance abuse (5). These are called the "Five Precepts" which one is to live by. These are not considered commandments, just good rules to live by. To discipline the mind, one should always look at things in a positive light and avoid negative thoughts. One should also practice meditation to sharpen awareness of the world and the self. Lastly, one should shed attachments.

If all of this is done properly, one may realize an awakened understanding and the wisdom one attains at the end of the path, nibbana.

After the Buddha's death, many different forms of Buddhism emerged; however, today only three major ones survive: Theravada, practiced primarily in southeast Asia; Mahayana, which developed in northern India but soon went east to China and other points east; and lastly Vajrayana, which flourished in Tibet and Mongolia. If it interests you, please feel free to research these forms on your own.

Please note that the Buddha's teaching did not provide for a foundation for a religion as we know it. He neither encouraged nor discouraged the belief in gods. He offered little in the way of worship, ritual practices and regular meetings or services. He believed that the pursuit of enlightenment was a personal path one had to take on their own. It was an inward journey of oneself and not a communal practice.

JAINISM

Out of northeastern India there arose another religion called Jainism, around the time of the Buddha, and modern history locates the origin of it in the same cultural environment that gave rise to classical Hinduism and Buddhism. Jainism was and is small in terms of followers but it had a tremendous influence on Indian history and religions. Similar to Buddhism and Hinduism as well, the most significant contribution of Jainism is its practice of ahimsa, which is the practice of not harming living beings. However, unlike Buddhism, the doctrines and practices of Jainism did not arise from one founder. With that said, there was one prominent sage, Vardhamana Mahavira, whose teachings shared much in common with the Dhamma or essential character of Buddhism and the philosophy of the Upanishads from Hinduism. Jains believe that Jainism is an eternal religion that has no beginning in time. When Mahavira taught the doctrines of Jainism, he was only transmitting a religion that was taught many times before by others. Jainism's teachers are called Tirthankaras, and their teachings show the way to salvation, which is the ultimate release from samsara. These people represent the highest possible attainment for the soul. There have been twenty-four Trithankaras so far, the most recent of whom is Mahavira, and it is believed that there will be twenty-four more in the current universal cycle. The next Trithankara is expected in 81,500 years.

The historical Mahavira was most likely born in 599 BCE in a royal household. At the age of thirty, Mahavira became a samana and renounced his kingdom and wealth. Like the Buddha, he practiced severe asceticism, including fasting, mortification, meditation, and silence. At age forty-two, he attained enlightenment and became the 24th Tirthankara and a "jina" which is a spiritual conqueror. His followers were called Jainas or Jains because they were disciples of the "jina." For the next thirty years, he traveled through the Ganges region teaching, until his death at about age seventy-two.

Like Buddhists and Hindus, the Jains appropriated the many beliefs circulating in the Ganges basin during the Indian Axial Age. However, Mahavira reinterpreted these to fit his own world view. Mahavira believed that the world was never created, because it always existed and will never be destroyed. He believed that the world goes through cycles. Each cycle is divided in half where there is a period of ascendency and then a period of decline. During the period of ascendancy people are tall, wise, just, and virtuous. As the cycle continues, people succumb to corruption and become shorter. At the lowest point in the cycle, people only live to twenty years old and live in caves, pursuing immoral activity. At the very lowest point, the cycle then turns around and a period of ascendancy begins. These cycles repeat endlessly.

Mahavira believed that the physical world was comprised of three levels: (1) the underworld where souls are punished to remove negative karma; when they have suffered enough, they are reborn into another realm; (2) the middle level, earth which is the home of life; and (3) the upper level, the home to the gods and where the Tirthankaras and the liberated souls dwell. He also believed like the sages of the Upanishads that the soul is real and unchanging in essence but not typical of a particular person. All souls are equal, and they are embodied in not only sentient but non-sentient beings as well. Jains believe that karma is a material substance that clings to the soul, staining and weighing it down. They believe that karma determines one's future births. They also believe that there are an infinite number of material and spiritual substances that affect us all. Because of this complexity and the limitations of human knowledge, they believe that all claims to what we hold as true are only tentative. This principle of "non-absolutism" means that we may be wrong about what we hold to be true. Jains believe that the path to salvation first means that one needs to stop the accumulation of new karma and then secondly eliminate old karma that is weighing down the soul. How do you do that? Well, do not harm other beings, practice right thought and right speech, do not take anything that is not yours, practice non-attachment (don't attach yourself to the things of this world) , practice chastity, meditate, perform penance, perform yoga, study and recite the sacred writings of scripture such as the Agam Sutras which is one of the most important Jain scriptures as a few examples. Now, where have we heard something similar to this?

There are some differences in Jain philosophy, but all Jains agree on the central message of non-violence, non-absolutism, and non-attachment. These practices are the basic elements for personal liberation from samsara and the collective goal for peace for the world.

Well, this completes the study of the main religions in South Asia which we can pinpoint primarily to India today. I hope you found that these religions of Hinduism, Buddhism, and Jainism provided a new and colorful insight as well as a jolt to your Western sensibilities (if you are Western) and your concept of religion. Also, I hope you take from this how these religions are quite similar in many respects, such as the concept of rebirth and the release from samsara. People share ideas and beliefs. It's just part of human nature.

We will now move on to the religions of East Asia, which will provide yet another perspective on religions of the world.

EAST ASIA BEFORE THE AXIAL AGE

For our spiritual journey in East Asia we should look at religion and culture prior to the Axial Age to help us understand the changes that were brought about by the Axial Age in that region. The focus here in East Asia will primarily be on China, where most of the changes during the Axial Age occurred.

The Chinese trace their history back 5,000 years. Over most of its recorded history, China has been the home of three major religions: Confucianism, Daoism, and Buddhism. We have already covered Buddhism, so our focus will be on Confucianism and Daoism. During these ancient eras, the basic features of Chinese civilization were established. These features were hunting and fishing for food, agriculture for crops, the use of boats and carts for transportation, religious rituals, the development of silk, central governments for organization, and the use of writing. These ancient eras hold important symbolic value to the Chinese, and they provide the measuring stick for future people to judge their values and behavior. Using the past as a moral yardstick can sometimes show that contemporary life may be lacking; as you will see later, there were some wise men in China who used this yardstick to point people in a better direction during the Axial Age.

The Shang Dynasty is the earliest period that can historically be substantiated in Chinese history arising during the 14th or 15th century BCE. It was discovered during 19th-century research that Shang kings were using the shoulder blades of cattle and the shells of tortoises to communicate with their gods and ancestors. These bones and shells would be inscribed with questions that were important to them, such as: What is the best time to plant crops? Why had someone become sick? What is the meaning of a dream? etc. Once the bones had been inscribed, the bones were heated or burned, which would result in cracks. These cracks would then be interpreted for answers to their questions from their gods. This process would be repeated several times to ensure accuracy.

These ancient people believed there was a close connection between the spirit realm (heaven) and the human realm (earth). Religious and political matters were also intimately connected, and no one would think of separating the two. In Chinese thought, the heavens and earth are continuous realms where the gods were always available to humans. Preserving the harmony between these two realms was of the upmost importance to the Chinese, and it was one of the king's principal duties. In Shang theology, the divine was composed of a heavenly court of gods, led by the Lord Supreme, Shang Di. This court mirrored the court of the kings on earth. The relationship between the gods and humans was strictly business-related. Humans would present the gods with pleasing sacrifices and tributes, and the gods would provide divine guidance and assistance with worldly matters for the humans.

Another big part of the beliefs of these ancient people, as well as the Chinese of today, was the role that their ancestors played. They believed that their ancestors mediated and conferred with the gods and could act on humans' behalf. It was also believed that the ancestors of the kings on earth would have an "extra" say and bend the ear of the Lord Supreme, Shang Di. In general, people thought it was very important to keep their ancestors happy so that they could appeal to them for favors because of their association with the gods, but I also feel that people felt it was best to remember and honor their ancestors because it was done out of love and respect for the ones that came before them which brings us to their belief in "De," which can loosely be interpreted as "virtue." It was believed that virtuous acts would generate a kind of power or force that would be pleasing to the gods or ancestors. This virtue had a power to effect people in a positive way, and it would compel the receiver to repay with a similar act of kindness

GETTING STARTED WITH THE RELIGIONS OF THE AXIAL AGE

called "bao." According to the ancient understanding of virtue, children are greatly indebted to their parents for giving them life. This is a debt that can never be repaid; therefore the only response is reverence for one's parents. The act of including ancestors in the ongoing life of a family is called "filial piety," and this reverence has been a foundation for Chinese culture before the Axial Age, during the Axial Age, and in today's culture of China. It can be seen that many aspects of the Shang Dynasty have endured in some fashion throughout much of Chinese religious history.

水 CONFUCIUS

Around 1045 BCE, the Shang Dynasty was uprooted by the Zhou Dynasty, which lasted until 221 BCE, when it was supplanted by the Qin Dynasty. This places the Zhou Dynasty right during the Axial Age. As in the time before, the people worshiped many gods, but the Zhou had a high god called Tian. In the Shang Dynasty, Tian was considered the "heavenly realm," but the Zhous personified Tian to be a personal god. In the Shang Dynasty, the gods did not care about how the humans behaved, either good or bad. However, the Zhous' Tian was concerned with humans' moral behavior. Out of this belief came a new concept the "Mandate of Heaven," or as it was called, "Tianming." It was decreed that the ruler governed with divine blessing as long as he was virtuous. This was the ruler's mandate to the gods. The Mandate of Heaven, however, was not universally accepted. The common people had an issue with gods being all good or virtuous. They saw the theological problem which plagues many people around the world to this day of evil as being contrary to the virtue of the gods. How can the gods be all good and powerful when evil exits in the world? If the gods are all good and powerful, wouldn't they have eliminated evil in the world? Dissent from the Zhou theology probably then was a matter of social status. The privileged and wealthy may view heaven and the gods as just and benevolent because of their safe and enjoyable life; however, the common folk who have to struggle every day for food and shelter may reject the idea of moral gods. Despite the Mandate of Heaven and the fact that the Zhou dynasty lasted the longest of China's dynasties (800 years), rifts began to appear. In 771 BCE, the Zhou king was murdered by invading nomads, and thus there entered a period of about 550 years of instability first and then toward the later part of the period—war. There was chaos during this "Period of Warring States," as it was called. The period was particularly disruptive and brutal, but out of this chaos came creativity from a philosophical and religious standpoint. As a result, intellectuals began to address the pressing issue of the day: How can people get along with one another? As a result, this warring period was also called the "Period of One Hundred Philosophers" trying to find answers to that pressing question.

Out of this political and brutal upheaval and period of philosophical creativity there entered China's most important Axial Age figure: Confucius. It is said that he was born in 551 BCE and died in c. 479. However, there are some historians that believe he was not a historical figure but rather a literary invention symbolizing certain values of the elite. For our purposes here, we will consider him as a primary figure of the Axial Age. The name Confucius was coined by Jesuit missionaries in the 17th century. In China he was known as Kongzi or Master Kong. He was born into the lower nobility and was a dedicated student. His father died when he was three years old. He was a man of great humility who was more concerned with self-improvement than with judging others. He was passionate about the arts. He believed that music had a moral dimension and listening to appropriate music could make one a better person. Confucius aspired to gain political power, but alas, it was not to be, so Confucius respected authority and believed that the key to human harmony lay in good government and in the moral character of the ruler and other public servants. If the leader is virtuous, then the people will follow suit. Therefore, he felt that people in power had an important obligation to always do what was right and virtuous.

Most of what we know about Confucius comes from the Analects (Lunyu) compiled after his death with his sayings, conversations, and anecdotes. No one knows to what extent the Analects are historically reliable, but most agree that much of it reflects the perspectives and words of his followers. Confucius thought that "tian" or heaven authorized him to teach and he applied the Mandate of Heaven to his work. However, it is important to note that Confucian thought is not founded on a particular vision of the divine, but rather on human potentiality. Can we then wonder, should Confucianism be considered a religion if there isn't much emphasis on the divine? Is it then inappropriate to think of it as a religion because of Confucius' emphasis on the practice of ritual and on the ancient religious forms? Please recall from earlier that Buddhism has a certain disinterest in gods and the spirit world as well, yet Buddhism is considered a major world religion. It is just my opinion, but if there is reverence paid to a particular moral ideal, then I think it can be labeled a religion. Confucius certainly had moral ideals. He urged people to practice goodness and kindness. He stressed that people should try and become the ideal gentleman or superior man, the "junzi," as it is called. This ideal man should strive to attain a noble character and superior status obtained by hard work and not by birthright. His teachings center on the character of a man and not his actions. However, he said that acting in ethical ways was fundamental in shaping one's moral character. What distinguished a gentleman from others was his "humaneness" or "humanity," called "ren." He was distinguished by his kindness, benevolence, and goodness. Ren is a virtue to be aspired to. Confucius said that the humane person acts to promote the success of others. Also, the desire to have other people fail is a major obstacle to realizing our full humanity. Confucius believed that the family is where we learn to love; however, we should love others only in proportion to the benefit that we receive from them. This last statement I find troubling, because in my opinion, it diminishes a person's "ren," but it is what it is. He believed in filial piety and reverence. Confucius believed that the gentleman should be compassionate but wise, know right from wrong, be a good judge of character, not blindly follow others, and possess self-knowledge. The disciples of Confucius found the path to goodness a difficult path to follow, but Confucius never promised a conclusion to following his way. It was not like Buddhism, where following the path could lead to enlightenment and the liberation of the soul. Those who take the path of Confucius for cultivating goodness did so only for its own sake.

Confucius believed that kindness and compassion required cultivation, and he provided guideposts for virtue called "dao" or "the Way." He believed in restraint. Don't eat too much. Don't get too comfortable. Meditate on personal thoughts and experiences. Wear the proper clothes as defined by the Analects. Detach yourself from your possessions. Practice good manners. Self-cultivate the proper observance of "Li," or the discipline of refining one's humaneness. Rituals were developed for this purpose and the gods were invited. These rituals were to put people in the proper state of mind and subordinate one's personal desires and needs. Confucius believed that by practicing virtue, one might accumulate enough virtuous energy to inspire others to be virtuous. He believed that this virtuous energy created by people could go up the social ladder as well as down, thus inspiring all to lead a proper and virtuous life.

After Confucius' death, his teachings were interpreted by his followers. There were two important philosophers that came after him, Mengzi and Xunzi, who agreed on many of Confucius' teachings but disagreed on the quality of human nature. Mengzi argued for the innate goodness of human nature, but Xunzi believed that human nature was neither good nor evil and that one's innate nature of goodness needed to be refined through ritual and practice. Their debate arose because Confucius was ambiguous on the point of human nature. This debate was at the crux of what many Axial Age thinkers were preoccupied with during this time. Please recall that Zoroaster believed that people had to lead their lives in either a good or evil way by making choices, and that the choices they made determined their individual destiny. Zoroaster's thought on this subject isn't quite the same as defining whether the "nature" of man is good or evil, but in a pre-Axial Age way it at least identified man as either good or evil, which in a way paved the way for more thought on this matter. Confucianism waned during the Qin Dynasty, which focused on legalism and embraced military and police force to keep order, but when the Han Dynasty came into power around 200 BCE, Confucianism was once again favored. Over the centuries, Confucius' prestige has waxed and waned, but overall, the Chinese have overwhelmingly admired him. All in all, Confucius was a good advocate of ideal moral behavior, and following his guidance would certainly lead to a better and more civilized society, don't you think?

DAOISM

We now turn to Daoism, which arose in China around the 3rd or 4th century BCE in response to the same upheaval in social and political conditions that supported the rise of Confucianism. It is said an elder contemporary of Confucius, Laozi, wrote the principal text of Daoism, called the Daodejing, however this is disputed. Some think that Laozi was a creation to provide an author for the work. In the text there are stylistic and linguistic differences that may indicate that many minds were at work in the writing of the Daodejing. In any event, that the work was probably written after Confucianism was established because much of the text clearly refutes central Confucian ideals.

The Daodejing, which is also called the Laozi, is a text that is hard to interpret because of its poetic and evocative style as well as its elusive subject. The Daodejing uses "Dao" to mean the ideal way or the way of nature, as well as meaning the universe's mother who is the source of all things that sustains and nurtures. However, it does not mean that Dao is a god or goddess. The Daodejing states that there are two aspects of Dao: one that can be talked about and one that cannot be talked about, so the human understanding of the Dao is limited. This twofold nature of Dao helps explain a paradox that runs through it. At times Dao is said to be stable, eternal, and constant. At other times it is described as the source of change or even perhaps it is change itself. The Chinese concept of yin and yang seems to shed a little light on this subject which is represented by the swirl of black and white that represents this concept. The Yin swirl represents the dark, hidden, passive, receptive, yielding, cool, soft and feminine. The yang swirl represents the light, open, active, aggressive, controlling, hot, hard, and masculine. This symbol represents the Chinese ideal of harmony and wholeness, suggesting that each thing requires its equal and opposite to maintain balance. Neither yin or yang can exist without the other. Each contains the seed of the other within it. This relationship accounts for the phenomenon of change, each giving rise to the other. Dao causes, or perhaps we can say is, change in the world. Simultaneously, Dao is the source of balance, harmony, and wholeness. Daoists believed that to neglect the way of nature and the universe is the root of society's misery. One should be flexible, yielding, and compliant, as water flows around a rock in a stream. One should look at what is not there, such as an empty room, and value what appears to be valueless. One should diminish the ego and its cravings for attention, recognition, and control. One should lose one's sense of self to experience a greater sense of reality. One should avoid dualisms of good and bad, right and wrong, beautiful and ugly, praise and blame. Systems of value are human constructions and should be avoided.

The Daodejing was originally intended to offer advice on how to manage government; however, as you can see from the above, it also offers help in managing one's own life as well. This convergence of achieving political and spiritual excellence is seen in the mystical practice of "wu wei." It is often translated as non-action, but one should think of wu wei as "actionless action" or "acting by not acting." To us lay people, we could say that we should act in the easiest way possible to accomplish what needs to be done which may also have the appearance of not acting at all. Humans have a compulsive desire to control, but this is not in accord with Dao. We want to regulate the course of our lives, rid ourselves of unpleasant situations, and coerce others to do what we want. The practice of wu wei is to relinquish ourselves of these desires. To practice wu wei is to practice non-interference and leave things alone. It is believed that if we do this, then everyone will benefit. One classic follower and philosopher of Daoism was Zhuangzi, who wrote a book also titled the Zhuangzi. One fundamental part of Daoism was the acceptance of change without resistance. In the Zhuangzi, he cautions against resistance and invites people to welcome the impermanence of life and to accept death as vital to happiness in life.

Daoism spread throughout China over the ages and became intertwined among the people's folk religions and practices. It is interesting to note that in China Daoism had periods of prominence and then periods of decline, usually when Confucianism was in ascendancy. Such is the way of Daoism – just leave things alone and let it be.

SOME THOUGHTS ON THE AXIAL AGE

I find the Axial Age a fascinating time and Professor Mark W. Muesse of Rhodes College provided a great course to provide an understanding of this age through the lens of history, which is where I drew my material for this age. I hope I did it justice.

Many religions which developed during that time emerged from a period where religions were primarily about rituals for having a good and fruitful life. Yet, the situation during that age was ripe for the people to want something more spiritually. In the case of Hinduism, people wondered about the significance of life and death and what it all means to humans. The Buddha observed suffering and out of his observations developed a course of action to reduce the suffering. In East Asia it was a time of war and some wise men asked themselves, "Is there more to life?"

However, what can we say about those Axial Age religions in general? Well, first of all, they were different in many ways, which points to the nature of man to adapt his beliefs to his personal experiences, environments, feelings, and thoughts. However, there seem to be cases where each religion adopted an aspect of another religion. Perhaps they influenced each other, or perhaps they developed certain aspects independently from each other. In any case, Buddhism and Hinduism share the concept of samsara and the concept of rebirth. Confucianism and Daoism both ascribed to the belief that governments should act in the best interest of the people, because each emerged due to trying times where there was lawlessness and wars. Each of these two religions addressed the need to provide good and just governments to best take care of the needs of the people.

However, the most important point of the Axial Age was that these religions emerged with an emphasis of looking at oneself. The "self" was recognized as a separate and important individual with moral responsibility. Issues were addressed such as lawlessness, selfishness, negative actions, suffering, what is the ultimate reality - among a few. Isn't it wonderful to think that between 800 – 200 BCE man was advancing from a focus on just living an everyday life to that of real thought about his existence in the world and universe and what his actions should be not just for his benefit but for his fellow man as well? I would say that the Axial Age was a time where the nature of man was maturing and that is a wonderful thing.

THE EVOLUTION OF GOD
BY ROBERT WRIGHT

*B*efore I found out about all the wealth of information in The Great Courses. I was talking with my daughter, Angelee, about this subject and she recommended that I read *The Evolution of God*, written by Robert Wright. It covers various religious beliefs and thoughts, but its primary focus is on the Abrahamic religions of Judaism, Christianity, and Islam.

I looked up Robert Wright on Wikipedia. Robert Wright (born January 15, 1957) is an American journalist and author who writes about science, history, politics, and religion. Wright attended Texas Christian University for a year in the late 1970s, before transferring to Princeton University to study sociobiology. He contributes frequently to *The New York Times*, and Wright became a senior editor of *The Atlantic* on January 1, 2012. In early 2000, Wright began teaching at Princeton University and the University of Pennsylvania, teaching a graduate seminar called "Religion and Human Nature" and an undergraduate course called "The Evolution of Religion." At Princeton, Wright was a

Laurence S. Rockefeller Visiting Fellow and began co-teaching a graduate seminar with Peter Singer on the biological basis of moral intuition. The Evolution of God was one of three finalists for the 2010 Pulitzer Prize for General Non-Fiction.

Well, it certainly seems that he is qualified to present to us his thoughts on religion. So, let's go!

First, I need to mention that I will be presenting the information from Robert Wright's book in pieces. Most of the information on the religions of Judaism, Christianity, and Islam will be presented in each of their respective sections that follow. The rest of my review and research on the book I will present here.

Robert Wright describes many times the religions or beliefs in his book as zero-sum or non-zero sum, which I paraphrase below in my own words as it relates to religions and gods, because you will see that I use these terms at times as we go forward from here.

Zero sum: implies an intolerance for other people's gods and beliefs

Non-zero sum: implies a tolerance for other people's gods and beliefs, regardless of whether it is for political or economic stability or gain.

His book mainly presents the Abrahamic religions of Judaism, Christianity, and Islam. These three religions all started their story with Abraham, his family and followers from ancient times. We will learn more detail about these important religions shortly.

In the meantime, we see the Abrahamic God(s) through the lens of their religious scriptures grow and change morally for the "good" of people. Could this be because of the "non-zero sum" breadth of mankind because we have to cooperate and tolerate other people and nations for our own well-being economically and otherwise? If you answer "yes," perhaps then it appears that you accept that the true nature of mankind is non-zero sum. Can we really say that it is? Are there exceptions? Remember, evil things happen in the world. This is something we all need to acknowledge.

Robert Wright points out that in past times, various hunter and gatherer groups, chiefdoms, and states developed and created gods that suited their own needs, such as gods to provide good crops, prosperity, status, goods, land, etc. as we have already seen. There were gods that were altruistic, such as Aten of the ancient Egyptians, but in early human development, most gods met the immediate needs of the various peoples and their rulers. Some rulers would occasionally use gods to strike fear into their people to suit their own needs. These rulers and shamans used visions to express the will of the gods. Often, these visions were induced through altered states, such as entering into trances.

In the ancient world, thought was given to the place of God in the world. Robert Wright mentions that there was a man that lived in Egypt between 25 BCE and 50 CE. He was called Philo of Alexandria. He lived under Roman rule. He used philosophical allegory in an attempt to fuse and harmonize Greek philosophy with Jewish philosophy.

Philo believed that there had to be reasoning between the scientific world of the Greeks in Athens and the religious world of Jerusalem. Both had to co-exist together (non-zero sum), otherwise God might eventually cease to exist in people's minds. There had to be intellectual reasoning between the secular and religious for this coexistence.

It is pointed out how Philo personally thought that God and man interacted. He thought that there was a sort of "ether" called Logos that permeated the world, if not the universe, that allowed man to "feel" God's intent for us. Let's call it wisdom.

This wisdom, when man connected with it, would allow him to see that cooperation with people who are different than we are would create an environment that would allow all to flourish. If this is so, it appears that this wisdom leads man to the conclusion that cooperation and love is part of the true nature of God.

There will always be conflict and violence in the world when selfishness and greed cause man to be insular; however, there is the implication that overall, when man connects with this wisdom as a whole, mankind will not be self-serving but cooperative, benevolent, and kind.

We even see this influence in Christianity in the book of John from the Bible's New Testament. Here Logos was replaced by the "Word," i.e. "In the beginning there was the Word." It appears that the author understood the nature of Logos and the importance of wisdom in order to connect with God.

Is this connection to wisdom similar to what Buddhists try to achieve when they meditate to attain Nirvana? Perhaps it is.

It appears that the nature of many men is to find their place in the universe. To do this, man must "think" to gain wisdom. If he is successful, he will see his place in the universe and be able to perhaps understand the true nature of God and the universe. Basically, it takes a lot of hard work and meditation to come to an understanding of oneself, God, and the universe. It is not given to you; you must work for it. I am just starting on this journey. I probably will never know enlightenment, but I hope this journey will enlighten me in some way.

For those that have gained this wisdom, can they answer whether the nature of the universe is more non-zero sum than zero sum? Is it more cooperative than insular? Is it something else? Can the tide of the universe shift one way or the other way? We have all seen the fluctuations of the

38

stock markets over the years. The stock market is a little microcosm of the universe in a way. People invest for all reasons. Some invest selfishly. Others invest for the betterment of others as well as themselves. Can we equate the Bull and Bear markets and the ups and downs of the market as a shift from non-zero sum to zero sum and back, in some way? If we can make this analogy, then perhaps the nature of the universe can have these tidal shifts one way and then the other. Perhaps the nature of the universe is not either non-zero sum or zero sum. Maybe the universe is what it is. Perhaps the universe doesn't take sides, and we just have to live our lives in whatever environment we have now.

Personal salvation may be tied to social salvation in a non-zero sum way. Goodness for the whole is good for you. However, different people interpret their religious scriptures in different ways. Some people that are oppressed may interpret it in a much different way than others and a zero sum approach to them may be better—an "all for me" approach. Environment certainly shapes people's beliefs.

Globalization of commerce seems to promote a non-zero sum society. For example, you need a car, and the people who make the car need your money, etc.

The problem is that people tend to distrust others. We are wired since prehistoric times to act in self-preservation, as the hunter-gathers of ancient times acted. If we see people demeaning others, we will naturally distrust them. Much of what we see in the west about Muslims is negative—burning flags, killing Westerners, etc. This is presented on the news all the time. However, it raises the question, if the news projected Muslims in a more non-zero sum way, would the West identify with the majority of Muslims in a non-zero sum way and realize that the terrorists are just a small minority? We are a product of our news media in that sense. Hatred blocks our moral imagination and our ability to put ourselves in the shoes of others.

Steven Weinberg, Nobel Prize-winning physicist, said: "The more the universe seems comprehensible, the more it seems pointless… It's not a moral order out there, it's something we impose."

However, there seems to be some sort of a moral order, because to not have an ever-widening circle of "acceptance" of others then there will be a price to be paid—instability, zero-sum, war, etc. It behooves humans to have a moral imagination to put themselves into others' shoes because it is in their best interest.

So, is the belief in God the "moral axis of the universe"? That is a good question.

Today, the Abrahamic religions still have a sense of uniqueness—a feeling that each is the favorite of God or the universe. In order to really grow these religions and all religions in general need to grow together in a non-zero sum way. They need to be humble.

Ashoka, who was a Buddhist, said, "If man extols his own faith and disparages another because of devotion to his own and because he wants to glorify it, he seriously injures his own faith."

The Hindus have a way of uniting many gods in their religion. The idea is that all gods, with their different names, are manifestations of a single Godhead. There are many gods, but can we say that they are part of One? Is the energy of the universe this One? If you think about it, there are probably as many religions and gods as there are humans. Each person takes their religion and probably tailors it to their own beliefs and experiences. This is not a bad thing. Who said that any one religion or religions are the best for mankind? We are all individual and provide our own moral imagination to the universe.

It is said that natural selection "invented" love. Creatures, including man, found that cooperating with each other was in their best interest in a non-zero sum way. So, are we heading to a non-zero sum global-ized society? That is the ultimate question for mankind.

Also, what is God? Is God love or something else? That question is what I want to try and answer on my journey, and I have a very long way to go.

Human beings make God into their likenesses and traits. It is then easier for us to understand and identify with God—a sort of personifi-cation of God. Xenophanes, a Greek poet, said that if horses had gods, those gods would look like horses.

The mind is built by natural selection, so people will do what they need to do to live and procreate even if it means believing and spreading false information. So, do we create our gods based on our own beliefs and prejudices? Good question. Is God really growing and changing, or is mankind "recreating" God in our minds as mankind changes? This is an important question. Do you believe that God exists? If not, then do you believe that God is the product of man's imagination, or do you believe something else?

In closing, I just want to provide you with a few thoughts. I briefly mentioned above that everyone takes their own personal beliefs and couples them with their own more formal and communal religious doctrines. I think this is a natural human tendency. We are all individu-als, and we want to form what we believe in a way that makes us feel comfortable. The formal religions of the world all mean well in their own way, but their doctrines are a way of telling a greater audience what they should do and believe. Most all religions at their core are good and just in a moral sense at least since the Axial age (800 – 200 BCE). Again, since all the great religions of the world are basically well intentioned, this isn't all that bad, but I think that the leaders of these religions have to understand that just maybe their way is not the way completely for each and every one of us. Each individual needs to build their beliefs on a foundation that is comfortable for them individually. For example, a Christian individual may believe in Jesus, the resurrection, the Holy Trinity, and life after death, but they may also subscribe to a Hindu belief in reincarnation and a caste system, in that they belong in a certain class of society and they are destined to stay in that class for their current lifetime. Is this a bad thing? I think it is not. We all need to feel comfortable in our individual beliefs. It is what makes us happy, and that is the important thing.

What if the leaders of the world's great religions embraced the above idea that religions are really individual? Would they quite possibly change their doctrines to embrace that idea? If so, then would these religions start to look a lot like the other religions, or quite different from each other? In the case that they started to look alike and there was tolerance for everyone's beliefs, could a new global religion start to emerge to replace the existing religions?

The above is an interesting thought, but I don't think it will ever happen. Religious leaders are basically set in their ways as it relates to their beliefs. I believe most people, to a certain extent, resist change, but isn't the above a very interesting thought? In any event, it's something that probably will never happen. There are far too many people in the world with far too many different ideas, and that is a lot of people to get on the same page and agree.

So far, I have touched upon the world religions of Judaism, Christianity and Islam. I don't know about you, but it makes me want to dig deeper into these religions and bring them alive in my mind. That is what I will do next.

Chapter 3

GREAT WORLD RELIGIONS

In my journey, I took a course called Great World Religions, which provides a very good overview of Judaism, Christianity, Islam, Hinduism, and Buddhism, as presented by five different professors. I have already covered Hinduism and Buddhism previously in my section on the religions of the Axial Age, so I will not repeat myself. However, I recommend this Great Course because it describes very well the main points of these five religions. Also, please note that I am not trying to go to any great lengths in my descriptions of these great world religions. My main purpose is to just give you the highlights and an overview of these religions in one condensed source of information so that if you find anything you want to research further, you can go off and continue your studies.

 JUDAISM

This particular Great Course was presented by Professor Isaiah M. Gafni of the Hebrew University in Jerusalem.

Judaism is a very ancient religion. It was started well before the Axial Age. Some say that it started when God presented the Ten Commandments to live by to the Jewish people from Mount Sinai, around 1400 BCE. Others say it started 4,000 years ago with the father of the Abrahamic religions, Abraham. In any case, Judaism is a very ancient religion that has successfully survived the test of time and is still going strong today.

To the Jewish people, Judaism is more than a religion. It is also a way of life, and it is a nation of people. It has geographical roots in the Middle East. The kingdom of Israel was founded by King David and lasted for about four centuries. King David was a descendant of the tribe of Judah, and the kingdom of Israel would thus be called Judah. Judaism identifies its historical roots in the Hebrew Bible, which Christians would later call the Old Testament. The Old Testament is defined as the Hebrew Bible, and it needs to be noted that throughout this work I use the term Bible without preface to mean the Christian Bible, which includes both the New and Old Testaments, where the Old Testament is from Judaism and the New Testament is a completely Christian book. In general, many of the faithful of each religion believe that both New and Old Testaments are the word of God given to man.

The Torah comprises the first five books of the Hebrew Bible. Hillel, a rabbinic sage from the 1st century BCE, replying to a convert's request for a crash course in Judaism, reduces the Torah to one principle: "What is hateful to you, do not do to your fellow man."

There have been attempts to define the essence of Judaism from the biblical texts. One common belief is that it can be defined by the Decalogue, which Christians call the Ten Commandments. The first five commandments deal with man's relationship to God, and the last five deal with man's relationship to man. However, some rabbinic figures think that doing this marginalizes the other parts of the Hebrew Bible. During the

Middle Ages, the search for the "roots" or essence of Judaism became more common. Confrontation with the Christian and Muslim worlds provided a need to distinguish and define the principles of Judaism.

In the 12th century, the Jewish philosopher Maimonides made an attempt at defining the principles of Judaism as a way of refuting major challenges posed by Christianity and Islam. The principles are as follows:

1) The existence of God. God's Unity (The belief that God is one).
2) God has no corporeal aspect (physical body or form).
3) God is eternal.
4) God alone and no intermediaries shall be worshiped.
5) Belief in prophecy.
6) Moses was the greatest of prophets.
7) All of the Torah in our possession is divine and was given through Moses.
8) The Torah will not be changed or superseded.
9) God knows the actions of man.
10) God rewards those who keeps the Torah and punishes those who transgress it.
11) Belief that the Messiah or savior will come.
12) Belief in the resurrection of the dead.

Maimonides stated that anyone who did not embrace these principles effectively removes himself from the Jewish community. The Jewish community basically embraced these principles, but as always, everyone has their own opinion and some tried to shorten, add, or just change some of the principles.

In the 18th century, many Western societies granted Jews equal rights while encouraging them to embrace their modern surroundings. Some

Jews downplayed their communal or nationalistic roots and stressed their religious roots. The result of this approach was either outright assimilation into the open society or a reforming of Jewish practice to make them more adaptable to modern surroundings. In the 19th century, the pendulum started to swing the other way, and there was a reawakening of nationalistic and ethnic roots out of which Zionism emerged and would have a great impact. Zionism is a movement to establish a Jewish nation in what is now Israel.

There is no doubt that historically, the Jews suffered great hardships over the ages. They were captives in Egypt, they suffered years on the move in order to reach the "Promised Land" that God promised to them, and once in the Promised Land, they were attacked by many enemies. They held to the belief that they were God's promised people even in the midst of defeat. They believed that their actions would either bring the wrath of God upon them or bring his blessings and prosperity. They were a people of deep ritual. For example, the book of Leviticus from the Hebrew or Jewish Bible preaches ritual, legal, and moral practices. Upon reading that book, you get a deep understanding that the Jewish people had to perform a lot of rituals daily. According to Wikipedia, the rituals, especially the sin and guilt offerings, provide the means to gain forgiveness for sins (Leviticus 4–5) and purification from impurities (Leviticus 11–16) so that God can continue to live in the Tabernacle (the portable dwelling place of their God, Yahweh) in the midst of the people. It must have been difficult to follow all those rules day in and day out without slipping up. The rules are very numerous and extensive.

In any event, the Jews did build their nation state, which lasted for years. They also built their temple in Jerusalem; however, the temple was destroyed in 586 BCE by the Babylonians, and the Jews were taken in captivity to Babylon. King Cyrus of Persia, after defeating the Babylonians, released the Jews back to their homeland, where they rebuilt the temple in Jerusalem only to have it destroyed again by the Romans in 70 CE. By the Middle Ages, the Jews were in all parts of the world and not just in their homeland. These Jews had to adapt to their new environments and live in coexistence with Christians and Muslims in many places. As stated above, the emergence of Zionism in the 19th century would have a great impact on the Jewish people, and the Holocaust that occurred in Europe during World War II helped fuel the need to establish a Zionist nation. Finally, in 1948, the Jewish people formed their nation when the state of Israel was established.

Robert Wright, from his book *The Evolution of God*, added a lot more detail about the Jewish people.

He stated that in ancient times, "holy" didn't have a connotation of moral goodness as it does today. At that time, it meant ritual purity, and according to the book of Leviticus in the Jewish Bible, ritual purity was of paramount importance.

For the ancient Jews, their God, Yahweh, was a warrior God. He struck fear into the hearts of the Jews and had them go to war for him many times.

Yahweh also chose the Jewish nation as his "people," where he led them out of Egypt and followed their every move during this Exodus. Yahweh was possessive and would punish them if they strayed from his ways. He was a jealous God that wanted them to worship only him.

It should be noted that the roots of ancient Israel came from poly-theism. Evidence is in the Old Testament, where in many parts of it, Yahweh is punishing the Jews for their worship of other gods like Baal (the god of the Caananites). Yahweh expected complete obedience.

In ancient Israel, many times good kings would lead the people on the right path to Yahweh, and likewise many kings led the people astray. In the latter case, Yahweh would provide their punishment. You can see evidence of this throughout the Old Testament.

In the journey of the Jews from polytheism, Josiah led Israel to mono-latry (the belief of only one true God without denying that other gods exist). He ruled with an iron fist. There was no tolerance for straying from Yahweh. This was the first step on the road to monotheism (the belief that there exists only one true God).

Does the road to monotheism necessarily mean that the believers in a god are intolerant of other people and their beliefs or as a minimum deny the beliefs of others? Consider how a great many Christians believe that the only road to heaven or God is to believe in Christ and the holy trinity. It raises the question: What about Muhammad's beliefs from the religion of Islam, Buddha's beliefs, the Hindu gods, etc.? These people also have formed a spiritual opinion about their reality of the world and how their spirituality fits into the whole pic-ture of the universe. In any event, it is a natural human tendency to embrace one's own beliefs and to deny, or at least disregard the beliefs of others.

Monotheism for the Jews grew out of the huge trauma they suffered as a people when the Babylonians exiled them to Babylon. This exile caused them to believe that Yahweh was a very strong God if he could turn and make the Babylonians punish the Jews for their indiscretions. This logic was convoluted, but it made sense to them at the time. The Jews then formed a strong identity with their God, the one and only God, and in a way, they were rewarded. They were eventually led out of exile, and they rebuilt their temple in Jerusalem. However, over time, the Jewish people would stray from their God at times, and they were provided with another reminder of Yahweh's strength when the Roman's destroyed their temple again in 70 AD.

✝ CHRISTIANITY

Now we move on to Christianity. This Great Course was presented by Professor Luke Timothy Johnson of Emory University. He is a former Benedictine monk and teacher at the Yale Divinity School.

Christianity began as a sect of Judaism in the 1ˢᵗ century CE. Unlike Judaism, Christianity did not make any claim to nationhood or a geographical area. However, it did and does want to recruit people to its ranks without regard to nationality or location in the world. In the beginning, Christians were persecuted by the Romans, but eventually the religion started to take root, primarily in Europe, and by the 4ᵗʰ century CE became the official religion of the Roman Empire under Emperor Constantine, whose conversion and edict of toleration in 313 CE, which is called "The Edict of Milan," reversed the political and cultural fortunes of Christianity. It is also one of the most paradoxical religions. Even though it makes no claims to nationhood, it was and is greatly involved in politics despite its primary message of peace and unity. It rejects worldly wisdom, yet it has claimed the allegiance of some great intellectual minds over the centuries. Christianity is a young religion. It is only about 2,000 years old. It is younger than Judaism, Hinduism, and Buddhism, but it is only a few centuries older than Islam. Over the last 2,000 years, Christianity has developed into three distinct groupings or forms which are: Orthodox, Roman Catholic, and Protestant. I will describe more about that later. However, within these groupings there are many different variations because of what I believe is man's nature to put their own individual stamp on their beliefs. Religion is important to people, and for that reason it is important to people to have their religion fit their ideal vision. I believe you can see this tendency of human nature in our study of the world's religions.

Christianity is one of the Abrahamic religions. Judaism and Islam are the other two religions. They are Abrahamic because the source of their lineage all start from Abraham and the lines of people that descended from his sons. We will also discuss this more when we get to our study of Islam.

However, it is important to note that the root of Christianity starts with Jesus of Nazareth, or Christ, as the Christians call him. He is not the founder of Christianity in the sense that Muhammad is the founder of Islam or that Prince Siddhattha is the founder of Buddhism, because this religion starts only after his death. He is the founder only in the sense that his resurrection from the dead gives birth to a religious movement that remains central to the Christian identity. When looking at Jesus, we need to look at him from two different standpoints: the historical and the religious. Primarily what we know of Jesus comes from the Gospels of Matthew, Mark, Luke, and John, whose narratives depend on an earlier oral tradition which are told from the perspective of Jesus as the Son of God. What we know historically is that Jesus' speech and actions identify him as a prophetic figure in the symbolic world of the Torah. Remember, Jesus did not see himself as Christian. He was a devoted Jew during his lifetime. It was only later that followers deified him on the road to the development of Christianity.

In the book *Zealot*, Reza Aslan sheds light on the historical Jesus. He was a preacher who launched a revolutionary movement which so threatened the establishment of the Jews and Rome that he was later executed. He was a man full of conviction and passion for his cause. In short, he was a revolutionary. He was a zealot. However, "the early Christian church preferred to promulgate an image of Jesus as a peaceful spiritual teacher rather than the politically conscious revolutionary." Will we ever know the true historical Jesus? I fear not. It is all a matter of faith and understanding what you want to believe about Jesus. Again, man shapes his vision of things in a way that will make him feel comfortable. Reza Aslan is certainly qualified to present his ideas to us. He holds a BA in religious studies from Santa Clara University, a Master of Theological Studies (MTS) from Harvard Divinity School, a Master of Fine Arts (MFA) in fiction writing from the University of Iowa's Writers' Workshop, and a PhD in sociology from the University of California, Santa Barbara.

In the second century, Gnosticism emerged. It was based on asceticism, the practice of self-denial; and cosmic dualism, the belief that the world is a struggle between good and evil. It was a very individualistic approach to Christianity. It preached that the material world is an imperfect creation of man and that the soul can transcend this material world through Gnostic knowledge. Many Gnostics rejected the current Christian writings of the day, such as the Gospels. As a result, the Gnostics did not fall in line with the mainstream development of Christianity in those early years. Gnosticism exists in modern times but is not a part of the mainstream Christian churches because of the public, institutional, and ritual nature of mainstream Christianity.

Part of the defining nature of Christianity is that to be a Christian means to share a story from beginning to end. Early Christianity has its roots in the Old Testament, which is part of their close relationship with Judaism. These stories tell of creation, the exodus of the Jews, the Promised Land, etc. It then continues with the New Testament and the story of Jesus, his followers and their beliefs, and then the formation of the church. It also tells the story of what is to come through the book of Revelation and the teachings of the various church scholars. This last part of the story is meant to inspire Christians to be good and to do good for others, because there is a hell as well as a heaven, and most people would not want to spend eternity in hell.

Christianity developed a very pronounced structure over time. The Christian Church developed a creed of beliefs to define what being a Christian meant. It defined moral criteria for people to live by. It developed sacraments to sanctify individual and communal life, such as the Eucharist (the body and blood of Christ), confirmation (becoming a member of the Church), matrimony, holy orders (the priesthood), penance (the forgiveness of sins) and the anointing of the sick. To other religions, the sacrament of the Eucharist might seem like a symbolic form of cannibalism, because during the service in church, the members are given bread and wine to consume, which represents the body and blood of Christ. This sacrament is supposed to bring the full "goodness" of Christ into the member's body, but to an outsider this might seem like a rather strange thing to do. However, as a Christian myself, I really don't think about the symbolic implications, because it is a ritual I have done for years. I just think of it as the goodness of Christ entering into my body.

In Christianity, a hierarchy of priests emerged in all three of its forms of Orthodox, Roman Catholic, and Protestant. In the early years, the church in Rome and Constantinople coexisted, but as time went on there were political and cultural differences between the Latin-speaking West (Rome) and the Greek- speaking East (Constantinople). Eventually, they split into what we know as Roman Catholic and Orthodox Christianity. Later in the West during the 16th century, there was reform to split from what was regarded as the corrupt Catholicism in the late-medieval period. As a result, Protestantism emerged. Again, there are many differences that distinguish each of these groups from each other, but my intent here is to just present an overview of the various religious beliefs of man and not present an in-depth study of the various religions.

However, I want to talk about the injustices done in the name of Christianity. In 1095 CE, Pope Urban II launched the First Crusade. In large part, it was done to unify Europe during a time of war and conflict, as well as a time where Muslims were overtaking the Holy Land. During the four Crusades, the Crusaders killed, tortured, and injured many Muslims, as well as people of different beliefs, primarily the Jews, on the way to the Holy Land. Additionally, the Inquisition in the name of the Church killed, tortured, and burned at the stake many people accused of heresy, as well as Jews, in an effort to keep the "Christian state" pure. I just want to mention this in the context of current-day Muslim Jihadists that capture, torture, and sometimes behead innocents today. Christians as well as many other faiths are certainly outraged by these brutal incidents today, but historically, during the Middle Ages, the Christians were just as brutal. All this was done in the name of the Church and God. Really? One could ask: Where was the humanity in mankind during those times?

Additionally, Robert Wright had a lot to add about Christianity in his book *The Evolution of God.*

He stated that there are inconsistencies in the New Testament which may or may not point to the truth or actual events. For example, Christ was crucified, but this goes against theological belief. Why kill the savior when he is supposed to save the world? However, it was justified as God sacrificing his only son and then raising him from the dead. Who would not be impressed by this from God? But does this bring us closer to knowing the truth about the life of Jesus?

Well, we know that Jesus was a Jew, and as such, when he referred to the "world," he probably meant Israel, because back then the world was much smaller to people, because they did not know the world was global. As such, he probably harbored traditional ideas about God and Israel.

Again, to this day we ask: What was the historical Jesus like? Well, I believe he was a man like all of us. He probably was a lot more energetic and devout than most. He was a Jew that believed in Jewish doctrines. He was driven to communicate his ideas. Was he God? Well, I think he was just like each and every one of us. Aren't we all a little part of God in our own way, if you believe in that philosophy? Perhaps he had more God-like qualities than we do, but I believe that the Jesus of Christianity probably has been embellished over the centuries to further the church, because it is what the Christians want to believe or actually believe that counts. I am not being judgmental on this point. I believe it to be the truth. Every human being brings a little bit of themselves to their own religious and spiritual beliefs, and perhaps that means embellishing the truth.

But what did Jesus do? Historically, the answer to the question is that probably we will never know that much about his real life, because there is very little historically written about him.

With that said, the book of Mark is probably more historically correct than the other Gospels. It was written closer to Jesus' life, but when people believe very strongly about something, there is a tendency to look past certain real events and present things in a way that supports their personal beliefs. When it comes to the Bible, we must bear that in mind.

In the Gospel of Mark, Jesus only uses the term "love" twice. However, Paul, who wasn't even one of the twelve apostles, uses the term very frequently after his conversion to Christianity. His conversion comes while on the road to Damascus one day; he saw a vision of a dead Jesus, and his motives of persecution of the Christians were questioned. Prior to his conversion, Paul was not a good person to Christians. He hunted them down, but then he saw the light and became one himself.

Paul taught "brotherly love." Paul's brotherly love was more a product of the environment of the Roman times than of Paul himself. People were moving to cities and away from their extended families. They would join groups such as the Christians for personal support, and to some extent, care. Paul capitalized on this to spread the word of Jesus. In a sense, he was "branding" his beliefs.

However, Paul had his restrictions; he would say that if anyone wasn't following Christian ways, they would be "accursed." Does this sound like an all-loving kind of God? Additionally, Paul really didn't get along all that well with the other apostles. Can you blame them for having trust issues? They were being hunted by Paul in an earlier time.

Paul's "brotherly love" was not universal. He did not want followers that were immoral, greedy, drunkards, robbers, etc. So, all were not included. Is this really "brotherly love"? Therefore, we can ask the question "What would Jesus do?" in this situation.

Despite Paul's restrictions, the New Testament's Pauline Epistles were not only for spreading the word of Jesus' love but a way of keeping his "brand" going in the places he had already visited and converted. He was a sort of CEO, and he had epistles at these places. He would write to them with advice and directions. He also used these letters to control "enthusiasts" that would stray out of bounds by doing things like speaking in tongues, etc. These letters were his form of "e-mail."

Paul's "business model" was to get all people to follow, whether they were Gentiles, Jews, or whatever. He had challenges, so he rejected parts of the Torah, such as dietary concerns and circumcision, which would not get the Gentiles to come into the fold. I guess it was a sort of "trade-off" to him.

Paul used business travelers to various parts of the empire to spread the word. This confederation, if you will, did provide a trusted network of reliable people. As his influence grew, there were many converts throughout the ancient world that could also provide lodging for other Christian travelers while away from their homes as well.

However, his message of brotherly love was spread throughout the ancient world of his time, and that should count for something in a non-zero sum sort of way. As history pushed the Christians to non-zero sum ways, which tended to lead them to moral improvement and moral truth, etc., then perhaps this also led them to believe in a higher purpose or a divinity? This is something for us to think about.

As I reflect on Paul's life, I see that he went through quite a transformation from a persecutor of Christians to spreading the word of Jesus throughout the Roman Empire. This is quite impressive, to be able to look inward to correct your perceived faults and then make such a dramatic change. I doubt if most people could make such a drastic transformation in their lifetimes. Whatever you think of Paul, you have to admit that his change and transformation was almost an impossible feat.

Robert Wright points out that Network Externalities is the making of a network of people larger where they all have a common purpose, such as a religion. This then will allow more information sharing. Basically, it is a large club with a common purpose. In theory, membership to a club should be easy to obtain, in order for the club to thrive and grow. If it is difficult to join, then probably a lot of people will give up and go away, and as a result, the club will not grow very much in size. Paul made his club membership easy. He accepted Jews, gentiles, and basically whoever wanted to join, except for the immoral, greedy, drunkards, robbers, etc., and that is why his form of Christianity has been the one to survive.

Here is a case in point. Marcionite Christianity was like Pauline Christianity, except that the founder, Marcion, rejected the laws of Judaism, whereas Paul did not. This restriction limited membership and is perhaps the reason why you don't hear much about Marcionite Christianity today.

There is an argument that even if Jesus hadn't been born, a similar religion would have grown eventually, such as what the Greek Apollonius of Tyana from Anatolia was preaching around the same time as Jesus. He preached that people should worry less about material things and more about the fate of their souls. It appears that the time was right for people to drift to a way that enlightened their hearts, and it appears that Paul, with his vast network in the Middle East and beyond, captured many hearts in the region.

In any event, it appears that religions compete with each other for members and recognition, and they probably always will. Is this because of a self-serving aspect of man? My way is the best way? There is also a "good Samaritan" nature to most men as well that needs to be considered. However, each man always feels that his way is the best when it comes to religious beliefs. Can it be said for each and every one us that no one should try and change what another believes, because what each individual believes spiritually is so personal? Is it at the core of their soul? We can speculate that there are probably as many spiritual beliefs as there are people on the earth. That's okay. One should believe whatever makes them feel comfortable and safe. However, is everyone's belief tied together through the universe partially, or in some way which doesn't contradict each other? Maybe, but if it is so, how? Perhaps it is people's image of their God that changes, not God. Would that help explain it?

During Jesus' life, the idea of a heaven wasn't fully formed, but it would be developed in the years afterward. The early Christians basically felt that after their death there would be a "rapture" or event on earth where the living and the dead that were good followers of Christianity would meet Jesus and live on earth for eternity. The idea of an afterlife was being formed, similar to the early Egyptian religion where a God called Osiris would judge the dead and determine their afterlife. In Christianity, if you are good here on earth, then you will have a good afterlife. This was a focal point of Jesus' teachings and why many viewed him then and today as a savior.

It should be noted that as civilizations flourish, religions evolve to provide a sort of order, or the right way to do things, which benefits both the individual and society as a whole. Religious rules are then established, such as to be "good" to everyone. Eventually this became associated with the afterlife, in that if you were good in life, then your afterlife would be enjoyable as well. We saw this in the section on the Axial Age.

ISLAM

Next, we move on to Islam. This Great Course was presented by Professor John L. Esposito of Georgetown University. He also serves a vital role as a consultant to the Department of State as well as a consultant to corporations and other governments on the subject of Islam. There is one editorial note that I want to mention. I am using Quran to mean the same as the term Koran. The usage is dependent upon my source of information. Here, Quran is used, but both terms are the same, where Koran is the Anglicized form.

The word Islam means "submission" or "surrender." Islam, like Judaism and Christianity, is a monotheistic religion, which is the belief in one God. Islam has more than 1 billion followers in some 56 countries, and it is the second-largest and one of the fastest-growing religions in the world. It is the second-largest in both Europe and America. It includes many peoples, races, languages, ethnic groups, tribes, and cultures. Only 20 percent of Muslims are Arabs. The majority of Muslims live in Asian and African societies. There is also a rich diversity of interpretation and cultural practices of Islam. However, a Muslim seeks to follow and actualize God's will in history, as an individual and as a member of a worldwide faith community.

Just like Judaism and Christianity, Muslims believe in angels, Satan, prophets, revelation, moral accountability and responsibility, divine judgment, and eternal reward or punishment. Islam is a dynamic religion that interfaces and sometimes competes with other religions. In contrast to the idea of separation of church and state here in America, many Muslims believe that religion and society, faith and power, are closely intertwined. Many believe that to be a Muslim is to live in an Islamic community-state governed by Islamic law. Additionally, the fact that many interpreters of Islam were males living in patriarchal societies certainly affected the development of Islamic law and thought, with a large "male centered" impact on women and the family, similar to the patriarchal influence on many other religions.

There is one Islam, as revealed in the Quran and the traditions of the prophet Muhammad, but Islamic tradition and heritage reveal many interpretations of Islam, some complementing each other, and others in conflict. Here again, man adds his own personal "flavor" to his religion.

Despite the enormous cultural, religious, and political differences, all practicing Muslims accept and follow the five pillars of faith. The first pillar is the declaration of faith. There is only one God, Allah, and that Muhammad is not only a prophet but the messenger of God to whom God has sent a book, the Quran, for the faith community. The second pillar is prayer, or salat. Muslims pray or worship five times a day, at daybreak, noon, mid-afternoon, sunset, and evening. In many Muslim countries, there is a call to prayer that sounds out over the rooftops, reminding everyone to pray. When they pray, they face Mecca. The third pillar is zakat, or tithe, which means purification. Zakat is both an individual and communal responsibility, expressing worship and thanksgiving to God to support the poor. It requires 2.5 percent of an individual's wealth and assets annually. Zakat is not considered charity. It is considered an obligation. It functions as a form of social security in a Muslim society. The fourth pillar is the fast of Ramadan. It occurs once a year during the month of Ramadan, which is the ninth month of the Islamic calendar. During the month-long fast, Muslims are required to abstain, health permitting, from food, drink and sexual activity from dawn to dusk. Fasting is not simply an act of self-denial. It is intended to stimulate religious reflection on human frailty and man's dependence on God. The fifth pillar is the pilgrimage or "hajj" to Mecca in Saudi Arabia. Once in every lifetime, a Muslim who is physically and financially able must make this pilgrimage totally in the service of God, to form one community of Muslims living their faith. The faithful should wear simple garments, which represent purity.

Jihad, which means to strive or struggle, is sometimes referred as the sixth pillar, although it has no official status. In general terms, Jihad refers to the obligation of Muslims both individually and communally to strive to do God's will, to lead a virtuous life, to fulfill the universal mission of Islam, and to spread the Islamic community. More specifically, Jihad means the defense of Islam called Holy War. Despite the fact that Jihad's purpose is to only defend Islam and not to include aggressive and offensive warfare, some Muslims have come to believe that it does.

Religion in pre-Islamic Arabia was tribal and basically concerned with everyday needs. There was little concern with moral responsibility.

Religion in those days was concerned with the needs of the individual, family, and tribe. There were many gods that were worshiped. Mecca was a rising commercial center during those early years and was a pilgrimage site for people to honor 360 different deities. As Mecca grew, so did the disparity between the rich and poor. This was the world that Muhammad was born into as a member of the most prominent tribe in Mecca, the Quraysh. However, he was orphaned at an early age and raised by his uncle, Abu Talib. He earned his living as a caravan business manager for a wealthy widow, Khadija, whom he later married. He was a man known for his integrity, trustworthiness, and reflective nature. He would often retreat to a hilltop in the desert to reflect on the meaning of life.

In 610 CE, during a night known in Muslim tradition as the "Night of Power and Excellence" Muhammad was called to be a prophet of God and later as the religio-political leader of a Muslim community-state. Over the course of more than twenty-two years, until his death in 632 CE, Muhammad received revelations from God through the angel Gabriel. These revelations would later be collected and compiled in the book known as the Quran. The Quranic universe consists of three realms – heaven, earth, and hell – in which there are two types of beings – humans and spirits. Spirits include angels, jinns (which are evil demons), and devils. Poverty and social justice are prominent themes in the Quran. It is the responsibility of Muslims to take care of the poor and disadvantaged. It is also their responsibility individually and communally to spread the word of God, Allah. The Quran also expresses pluralism and tolerance. God created many nations and people. Historically, although the early expansions and conquests spread Muslim rule, in general, Muslims did not try to impose their religion on others or force them to convert.

Another major message in the Quran is that men and women are equal and complimentary. They are each equal parts in a pair. However, I believe that the patriarchal nature of the early leaders and Muhammad himself may have influenced how parts of the Quran were actually written and interpreted in practice. There is one verse in the Quran 4:34 that says "Men have responsibility for and priority over women, since God has given some of them advantages over others because they should spend their wealth [for the support of women]." Additionally, the Quran advises Muhammad's wives to "stay in your homes," "not display your finery" and place a barrier between themselves and unrelated males. So, it appears that the issue of women is open to interpretation in Muslim communities. There are some Muslim countries where women can drive, vote, hold professional positions, serve as ambassadors, be parliamentary members, be judges, etc. Yet in other countries they can't drive, must be segregated from men, cannot vote, be covered in public, etc. I guess it depends on which Muslim country a woman is born into that determines her extent of personal freedom. However, it needs to be pointed out that in the most restrictive Muslim countries, not all women feel repressed. Many feel that it is a part of their culture, and they do not feel restricted. It is just part of their religion and an obligation to God that they should practice and obey these laws.

Muhammad's reformist message posed a particular struggle for the leaders and businessmen of his day. He denounced the status quo and called upon people to provide social justice for the most vulnerable in society: the poor, women, children, and orphans. His message was not received well in Mecca, and after some persecution and little progress, he moved to Medina. In Medina he was well received and served as prophet, political ruler, military commander, chief judge, and lawgiver of the Muslim community, which was composed of Muslims and non-Muslims. He allowed Jews and Christians their religious freedom as long as they paid a "poll tax" and were loyal to his government. Despite this, there were still some tensions, which were more political than religious, with the Jewish communities. Additionally, there were many battles Medina fought with Mecca, but in 628 CE a truce was struck, granting Muslims the right to pilgrimage to Mecca. Mecca was later subdued, and Muhammad consolidated Muslim rule throughout Arabia through a combination of diplomatic and military means.

After Muhammad passed away, leaders expanded Islamic law. Islamic law came to reflect Islam's emphasis on orthopraxy, which is **correct practice,** rather than orthodoxy or **correct belief.** Islamic law applies to both the private and public realms and is concerned with human interactions with God, Allah, and with social relations with each other.

Perhaps as a response to this orthopraxy, Sufism or Islamic mysticism emerged in response to the growing materialism and wealth that accompanied the expansion and growing power of the Islamic empire. Sufis found the emphasis on laws, rules, duties, and rights to be spiritually lacking. They instead emphasized the "interior path" of seeking purity and simplicity as the route to direct and personal experience of God. They pursued an ascetic lifestyle that emphasized detachment from the material world, repentance for sins, and the Last Judgment, which is the judging of the thoughts, words, and deeds of persons by God. Today, Sufism remains a strong spiritual presence and force in Muslim societies in both private and public life, enjoying a wide following in Europe and America, attracting many converts to Islam.

As a lay person to the religions of the world, Islam included, it appears to me that perhaps if Muhammad were alive today he would find the right balance between "right practice" and "right belief" for Islam. However, we will never know what his thoughts would be if he were to observe what his religion has become today.

Now, let's see what Robert Wright has to say about Islam from his book *The Evolution of God.*

Robert Wright pointed out that the Bible was written by many men and there were many years in the making of this book. However, it is thought that the main Islamic text, the Koran, was probably inspired by only one man, Muhammad, over the course of two decades. It is believed that the Koran was not physically written by Muhammad. Muhammad verbally presented what God had told to him, and his followers transcribed God's word. The writers of both documents were inspired by their religious zealousness, and they may have overlooked the reality they saw every day in their normal lives in favor of their personal beliefs about what they were writing. Since Muhammad was probably the primary inspiration for the written Koran, this work was therefore mainly influenced by his beliefs, whereas the Bible was written by many, and thus subject to the personal thoughts and beliefs of a great many men. In any case, one must be careful when reading these works and try and sift out what may actually be historically correct versus what is the belief of the authors.

As noted above from the book *Zealot* by Reza Aslan, we can speculate that the real Jesus was actually a revolutionary and zealot. With that said, we can speculate that if the "real" Jesus wrote the Bible, it probably would have the same flavor of fire and brimstone as parts of the Koran.

It is important to note that the God of Abraham and Jesus was also the God of Muhammad. Perhaps, Muhammad was influenced by his Christian cousin, which might help explain why this is the case. Additionally, Muhammad had a lot in common with Moses. Moses was outraged by how the Egyptians treated the Jews, and Muhammad was outraged by how the rich Arabs treated the poor Arabs.

Muhammad eventually moved to Medina, where Islam flourished, after he was shunned as a street prophet in Mecca. Medina was good to Muhammad, whereas Mecca was not.

Muhammad drew parallels between himself and both Moses and Jesus, because I'm sure they all thought of themselves as prophets of God. The Bible portrays Jesus' story in a positive light, but the Koran does not take poetic license in its portrayal of Muhammad's word from God as the Bible does of Jesus. The Koran is a story of "rejection." With this rejection, there is vacillation between its messages such as "kill infidels," mixed with preaching tolerance. Muhammad is just one man trying to reconcile his circumstances. Perhaps, the Koran documents his inward struggles with his polarized beliefs, at times. Could we attribute some of these differences in the Koran due to when and where he wrote the verses – in his Meccan years verses his Medina years? Perhaps we can.

In the Koran's Meccan writings, it is God who is to provide retribution to the unfaithful, not the Muslims. During Muhammad's Meccan years, he encourages people to resist the impulse for vengeance. Let God handle it. This is similar to the Christian writings to basically turn "the other cheek" after being abused and let God handle their judgment.

When Muhammad moved to Medina where the people were more tolerant of his beliefs, his preaching became more aggressive and less tolerant toward the Meccans. I guess your surroundings can determine, to a certain extent, your actions and beliefs. We all need to be aware of this as we form our own individual spiritual identities.

As the Bible also preaches, the Koran paints a picture that the faithful will be rewarded in the afterlife, while the unfaithful will be persecuted after death.

At one time, Muhammad wrote what were called the Satanic verses. The Satanic verses were part of the Koran until Muhammad realized that they were inspired by Satan and then he had them removed. Just like all of us, Muhammad had the ability to change and constantly evaluate himself and his beliefs. These verses describe the three daughters of Allah, but this put his monotheistic beliefs in jeopardy just to gain credibility (non-zero sum) with the pagans. He changed his mind and later removed those verses.

In Medina, Muhammad gained not only religious but political power. The prophet, Jesus, never had real political power, but what if he had? Would he have been tolerant of people of different religious beliefs? As a Christian myself, I would like to think he would have been tolerant, but since we don't really know the historical Jesus well, we will never know his personal motivations. It gets us thinking about prophets in general, and the possibility of them attaining some political power. It would be up to each individual prophet and their personal natures as formed by their experiences whether they would be just or unjust, tolerant or intolerant. They may be well intentioned when they have no political influence, but if they had power—what then? Power has a way of changing people. Other than Muhammad, we will never know what other prophets would have done, but hopefully they would have been tolerant of others.

In the quarter century after Muhammad left Mecca for Medina, his small tribe of believers became an Islamic state that overtook the Byzantine and Persian empires, as well as Egypt and Palestine. Muhammad's relations with the Christians and Jews in the area grew hostile, and in some cases, violent. He wasn't getting many converts, and Muhammad didn't view the Jews and Christian as completely monotheists.

Muhammad did try to get Christians and Jews to believe. He had the Muslims eschew pork, pray toward Jerusalem, and had a holy day called Yom Kippur. He believed that his Koran was where the Torah and Gospels would migrate to as a better word of God, if the Jewish and Christian leaders made an effort to make changes to their religious documents.

Muhammad in Mecca was a prophet. Muhammad in Medina was both a prophet and politician. In Medina, he worked to get the people to believe in his God as well as believe in him as God's prophet.

Muhammad led raids against Meccan caravans and eventually subdued the city of Mecca relatively peacefully because of his strength in numbers. He justified these actions by saying that those who were wronged could take action, and he felt he has been wronged by the Meccans.

Eventually, relations got worse with the Jews, and he made changes. He had Muslims now pray toward Mecca and no longer to Jerusalem. Eventually, Jerusalem was taken over by the Muslims in the 7th century. There is a Greek account that the Muslims and Jews banded together to capture the city; however, there is no real proof, especially in light of the fact that relations between Muslims and Jews were quite tense at times.

According to Muhammad, he had both Abraham and Ishmael end up in Mecca somehow and build the Ka'ba, which is the Islamic shrine. However, it is unknown who really built it.

Both the Muslims and the Jews came from descendants of Abraham (although the Jews felt that their descendants were more legitimate). Below are the family trees, according to what Muhammad has said.

Jewish descendants: Abraham -> Isaac (from his wife Sarah) --> Jews

Islamic descendants: Abraham -> Ishmael (from his slave Hagar) -> Muslims

Religions that reach great stature tend to rewrite their history in a favorable light as related to their beliefs. They also tend to find an epoch-marking figure such as Moses, Jesus, or Muhammad and turn them into that epoch-making figure. Again, people want to believe that their way is best. This is a normal human tendency, so they may take liberties and rewrite history in a slightly different way to accommodate their personal beliefs. They are not really trying to deceive anyone. They just believe. However, it may be that they are deceiving themselves in the end.

There is no "doctrine" of Jihad written in the Koran. However, people interpret what they want in their religious beliefs. Religions can be made peaceful or warlike, depending on what is in the hearts of the people.

Jihad implies a struggle. Is it meant to mean an outward and warring struggle, or an internal struggle with oneself? Again, a matter of interpretation as to which one you want to choose. I think Muslims actually mean both, based on whatever suits their needs at various times.

The Median parts of the Koran were aggressive in the context of war. Could Muhammad have perhaps been having a bad day? Maybe, but do you think that the individual writers of religious texts are putting their own thoughts into God's mouth? In any case, the Koran does use warring phrases, but it also expresses the idea not to harm infidels who mean no harm to you. Are current-day Jihadists taking a lot of the Islamic teachings out of context and using only what they want in order to support or point out their agenda? That is a good question.

Over the centuries, Muslims would interpret the Koran and hadith (the Muslim oral traditions and knowledge) according to their own needs on the ground. If they were in war, then they would justify their actions from the warring parts. If they are at peace, they would be much more tolerant of the infidels or non-believers.

Muhammad was political. After many great accomplishments for the Muslims, Muhammad died in the year 632 AD. He secured control of Medina and promoted his beliefs. Muhammad is an example of a prophet that gains power. You be the judge of whether he used his power wisely, just as I posed the question a few paragraphs ago as to whether Jesus would have used power wisely if he had it.

The Jewish Bible, Christian Bible, and the Koran all had a lot of hatred of infidels written into them, but in terms of salvation, Muhammad's Koran offers the chance of salvation to non-Muslims if they behave devotedly. Christianity preaches that salvation is open only to pious Christians.

Muhammad also believed that ecosystems are conducive to human flourishing by God's design. Therefore, like small organisms since the beginning of time, the global ecosystems on earth are like an organism. Humans are like the brain, plants and trees are like the lungs providing oxygen for the other living creatures, etc. It seems that we are a small part of a greater whole. Could it be that the whole is what we might call God? If you think of it in this way, don't you feel very small right now?

In any event, the religion and story of Islam is colorful, full of contradictions and piety all rolled up into one, and isn't that wonderful?

Chapter 4

LET'S DISCUSS WORLD RELIGIONS A LITTLE BIT MORE

BAHA'I FAITH

Fairly recently my uncle, Rollin E. Johnson, retired from his profession as a Protestant minister, and he asked me if I would like to go through his library and take any works that might interest me. I collected a number of works on religion and philosophy, but there was one very interesting pamphlet on the Baha'i faith. I was very intrigued by it, so I looked it up on Wikipedia at: https://simple.wikipedia.org/wiki/Bahá%27í_Faith

This is a short summary of some of the information in the article:

'The Bahá'í Faith is an Abrahamic religion started in the 1800s by an Iranian person called Bahá'u'lláh who was born in Tehran, Iran. Followers of this religion call themselves Bahá'ís....

Bahá'ís are monotheists, which means that they believe in one God. They believe Bahá'u'lláh carried a message from God. Bahá'u'lláh said he was not the only person to carry a message from God, and he was not the last to carry a message from God. He taught that the people who started the other major religions also represented and carried messages from God, such as Jesus, Moses, Abraham, Muhammad, the Buddha and others. He called these people "Manifestations of God." They believe the messages from the Manifestations of God get more and more difficult to understand.....

Because God is greater than the whole universe, Bahá'u'lláh said that human beings cannot completely know God. He said that God wants people to know as much about him as they can. Bahá'u'lláh wrote God sends special people to manifest (show) himself to ordinary humans. Without the Manifestations of God we could not know God. Bahá'ís believe the God they pray to is the same God Abraham spoke to, Jesus talked about, and Krishna said in Gita.....

Bahá'ís say that he is not the last prophet/manifestation of God. They think there will not be another prophet for 1,000 years after Baha'u'llah's death.....

Bahá'ís also believe that the Bible, the Qur'an, the Gita and other books from other religions are special.....

Some important Bahá'í beliefs are:

- Bahá'u'lláh came to make all humans become one family
- There is only One God, but he has many names

- All the great religions have the same source (God)
- God treats all humans as equal
- God treats men and women as equal
- Prejudices (unkind beliefs about people without knowing them first) should be fixed
- Nations should learn to get along and co-operate with each other
- Science and religion do not have to disagree, because they are looking at the same world from two different sides.
- People should try to learn the truth for themselves
- Everyone should get an education (go to school or learn another way)
- The world should have one extra language that everyone understands

There are eight or nine million Bahá'ís in the world, of all peoples and languages....

They do not have priests. Everyone is responsible for their own prayers. Bahá'ís are also responsible for reading their holy books for themselves and for learning about their religion. Baha'is elect leaders for their community, to help organize their activities, and to deal with problems between members, and to decide things that are not obvious from the scriptures. These are called Spiritual Assemblies, but will one day be called Houses of Justice.

There is one House of Justice, which Bahá'ís call the Universal House of Justice, which leads the whole worldwide Bahá'í community. Bahá'ís elect this House of Justice every five years, but only once each year for National and Local Spiritual Assemblies.'

It is interesting that this religion is called Abrahamic. We commonly think of Judaism, Christianity, and Islam as the only Abrahamic religions. I guess we can add this one to the list. But there is another interesting point. This religion was born in Iran. I find it interesting that this religion originated in about the same geographical area where the Axial Age religions originated. Is there "something in the water" there that inspires people spiritually? Interesting thought, but I think we will never know.

The thing I like about this religion is that it is very open and inclusive. Most everyone has a God, but in fact everyone's God is the same God. No one religion is better than another, and nations should be all- inclusive and altruistic. Men and women are equal. Everyone is equal. This religion believes in a kind of Utopia where everything is right with the world. I think I could get behind this religion. It sounds good for humanity.

ATHEISM AND AGNOSTICISM

This work would not be complete without talking about atheism. I looked it up on Wikipedia at this site:

https://simple.wikipedia.org/wiki/Atheism

Here is some of what it had to say:

'Atheism is rejecting the belief in a god or gods. It is the opposite of theism, which is the belief that at least one god exists. A person who rejects belief in gods is called an atheist. Theism is the belief in one or more gods. Adding an a, meaning "without", before the word theism results in atheism, or literally, "without theism".

Atheism is not the same as agnosticism: agnostics say that there is no way to know whether gods exist or not. Being an agnostic does not have to mean a person rejects or believes in god. Some agnostics are theists, believing in god. The theologian Kierkegaard is an example. Other agnostics are atheists. Gnosticism refers to a claim of knowledge. A gnostic has sufficient knowledge to make a claim. Adding an a, meaning "without", before the word gnostic results in agnostic, or literally, "without knowledge".

While theism refers to belief in one or more gods, gnosticism refers to knowledge. In practice, most people simply identify as a theist, atheist, or agnostic....

Anaxagoras was the first known atheist. He was an Ionian Greek, born in Clazomenae in what is now Asia Minor. He travelled to other Greek cities, and his ideas were well known in Athens. Socrates mentioned that his works could be bought in Athens for a drachma. Eventually he was prosecuted and condemned for impiety, and banished from Athens.....

Atheists often give reasons why they do not believe in a god or gods. Three of the reasons that they often give are the problem of evil, the argument from inconsistent revelations, and the argument from nonbelief. Not all atheists think these reasons provide complete proof that gods cannot exist, but these are the reasons given to support rejecting belief that gods exist.

Some atheists do not believe in any god because they feel that there is no evidence for any god nor gods and goddesses, so believing any type of theism means believing unproved assumptions. These atheists think a simpler explanation for everything is methodological naturalism which means that only natural things exist. Occam's razor shows simple explanations without many unproved guesses are more likely to be true.'

I want to clarify what the three reasons are that some atheists give for their non-belief in God as mentioned just above.

The problem of evil to atheists is that if God existed, then he would not allow evil.

The argument from inconsistent revelations is that some of the occurrences or revelations from the various world religions are inconsistent or contradictory.

The argument from nonbelief is that if God existed he would want humans to know it, but he hasn't made himself known.

Hopefully, this clarification helps. Overall, you will have to admit that the atheists have some very good arguments about the nonexistence of a God or gods.

Maybe the study of philosophy can help us understand this issue a bit more, which we will look at in a little while. However, we first need to address paganism.

PAGANISM

Paganism tends to scare quite a few people that follow other religions, but it should not. Many associate paganism with devil worship, but that is not correct. At the following website there is the following explanation written by Patti Wigington. Patti Wigington is a pagan author, educator, and licensed clergy. She is the author of *Daily Spellbook for the Good Witch*, *Wicca Practical Magic*, and *The Daily Spell Journal*.

https://www.learnreligions.com/do-pagans-worship-the-devil-2561845

> "Do Pagans really follow Satan? The short answer to that question is *No*. Satan is a Christian construct, and so he's outside of the spectrum of most Pagan belief systems…
>
> If someone tells you they're a Satanist, then they're a Satanist…
>
> It's also important to keep in mind that most people who self-identify as Satanists do not, in fact, worship Satan as a deity, but instead embrace a concept of individualism and ego. Many Satanists are in fact atheists…
>
> Many evangelical branches of Christianity warn members to avoid any sort of Pagan belief path. After all, they caution you, worship of any being other than the Christian god is tantamount to devil-worship. Focus On the Family, a fundamentalist Christian group, warns that if you're looking at the positive aspects of Paganism, it's because you've been tricked by the devil."

There you have it. Paganism is not Satanism. However, both appear to get a bad "rap" by some fundamentalist Christian groups.

So, what is paganism?

At the following Wikipedia website, this is what they have to say about paganism.

https://en.wikipedia.org/wiki/Paganism

'Paganism (from classical Latin pāgānus "rural, rustic," later "civilian") is a term first used in the fourth century by early Christians for people in the Roman Empire who practiced polytheism. This was either because they were increasingly rural and provincial relative to the Christian population, or because they were not milites Christi (soldiers of Christ). Alternate terms in Christian texts for the same group were hellene, gentile, and heathen. Ritual sacrifice was an integral part of ancient Graeco-Roman religion and was regarded as an indication of whether a person was pagan or Christian.

Paganism was originally a pejorative and derogatory term for polytheism, implying its inferiority. Paganism has broadly connoted the "religion of the peasantry". During and after the Middle Ages, the term paganism was applied to any unfamiliar religion, and the term presumed a belief in false god(s). Most modern pagan religions existing today (Modern or Neopaganism) express a world view that is pantheistic, polytheistic or animistic; but some are monotheistic.

The origin of the application of the term pagan to polytheism is debated. In the 19th century, paganism was adopted as a self-descriptor by members of various artistic groups inspired by the ancient world. In the 20th century, it came to be applied as a self-descriptor by practitioners of Modern Paganism, Neopagan movements and Polytheistic reconstructionists. Modern pagan traditions often incorporate beliefs or practices, such as nature worship, that are different from those in the largest world religions.

Contemporary knowledge of old pagan religions comes from several sources, including anthropological field research records, the evidence of archaeological artifacts, and the historical accounts of ancient writers regarding cultures known to Classical antiquity.'

It appears that paganism may be polytheistic, and it may involve the worship of nature. It is important to note that we all create our own spiritual and religious beliefs that suit our needs. Pagans are doing the same thing, and that is what makes them feel comfortable in their world.

SOME FINAL THOUGHTS ON THE WORLD'S RELIGIONS

*W*ell, we have finished our look at the various world religions, or as much as we are going to look at them in this study. There are many other world religions that we could review, but that would greatly increase the scope of this work. However, I think we have at least touched upon the most prominent religions over the course of time up to the present, and I think we now have a well-rounded overview of them at this point. It is time to move on to philosophy, but before we look at the world through the philosopher's lens in our next section, let's wrap up with some thoughts on the world's religions that we have studied.

Based on the way that I ended our study of the Axial Age, you would think that man now had turned a corner and was on the road to Utopia where all people cared about their neighbors and would work together for the best interest of all the people. Well, that did not happen, as you know, because not everyone was of the same opinion of the sages, shamans, and philosophers of that age. In any event, you could at least give those wise men an "A" for effort.

Wars were still fought by all nations after the Axial Age. The crusades of the Christians were certainly not an example of their best Christian behavior. Genocides of Armenians occurred in Turkey and surrounding regions of the Ottoman government around World War I. Genocides occurred in Europe during World War II, and in the Baltic states in the 1990s, just to name a few. Recently, terrorists have now targeted innocent people in the name of some cause or religion, just because someone somewhere didn't agree with them on some matter. It is just sad that for some people the value of human life is so low.

However, with that said, for a great many people—I would dare say the majority of people—life is important, which is why religion has played a large role in the lives of so many people over the ages. Whether religion served just the daily needs of the people or provided food for thought for their souls and afterlife – religion is important to man!

So, now that we have seen a sampling of what the more prominent world religions are like, what can we say about them?

We saw how the ancient Jewish God was a jealous God and required excessive rituals of obedience. He chose the Jewish people as his people. He wanted them to have no other gods. Exactly why were they the chosen ones? Were they better than other people? Or is it human nature to want to be special and the early Jews just declared that God liked them the best? However, we also see this in Christianity and Islam, where those religions also professed that their "way" was the best. We see this tendency in other religions as well. In Hinduism and Buddhism, we see that they don't reject other people because they believe differently, but they believe what they want to believe and practice their own rituals because to them it provides the "way" for them. I believe we can conclude that whatever religion a man follows, it is a personal choice for him and him alone. He makes his choices based on what makes him feel comfortable. Everyone is certainly influenced by their environment and the religions and beliefs of their parents, but ultimately, man needs to feel comfortable, and he may change his perceptions of his local religious world view to suit his personal needs.

We saw that at first gods were for the benefit of man in his daily life—good crops, safe trips to the next town, successful childbirths, etc. Later, we saw that man was not just satisfied with help from the gods in his everyday life from the gods. He wanted more. He saw himself as an individual person and started to wonder about his existence and place in the universe. It was then that he started to explore, in the recesses of his mind, his own meaning in life and ask some very tough questions. What would happen to him? Where would he go when he dies? Is there a heaven? If so, then if he is morally good, will it help him to get to heaven? If there is a heaven, what is it like? If there isn't a heaven, then what happens? Do his life and his soul end at death, and his existence as an individual end? Does God really exist?

These are some very deep and important questions that mankind has asked and still is asking. Quite frankly, the answers to these questions are rooted in faith and not in truth, as we will see in the next section on philosophy. We will never know the truthful answers to these questions, but each one of us can form an opinion that makes us feel comfortable with our destiny. That is faith, and that helps us put order and comfort in our lives. Yes, that is a good thing.

Now on to what philosophy can tell us about God, our souls, our free will, and our minds.

Philosophy

When I was in college, I focused my studies on mathematics and the sciences. In fact, I graduated with a bachelor's degree in mathematics from Norwich University in 1975. Since I was in the bachelor of science program, the required courses were primarily centered on math and the sciences with some history and English courses also required. Back at that time, I took a few elective courses in history and English, but I stayed away from the arts and philosophy, not because I didn't value them, but because as a young twentysomething, I wanted something practical that translated into career potential as I saw it at that time in my life. I was fairly good but not great in math, so I took that course of action. I think if I had wanted real career potential, I would have gone into one of the engineering majors instead of math, but at that time I lacked the wisdom that I have now from my life experiences. However, with that said, my math degree did serve me well in my career in information technology, but I really missed out on something that would become important to me later in life—real wisdom. At a ripe old age of sixty-four the study of philosophy finally entered my life. Up to that time, I thought that Philosophy was simply the beliefs that someone held on a particular subject and that was it in a nutshell. I never thought about whether those beliefs might or might not be grounded in facts or the truth. Well, I was soon educated in all matters philosophical.

THE BIG QUESTIONS
OF PHILOSOPHY

In 2017, I took a Great Course on The Big Questions of Philosophy, taught by David Kyle Johnson of King's College in Pennsylvania. At first, this course was hard for me to wrap my mind around because I was never made to think outside of anything in my "practical" life. The study of philosophy requires you to look at what your preconceived ideas are and examine them to see if they have some sort of validity. This course was "eye-opening" for me, and the instructor was young, new, fresh, and very well educated in his subject matter, and he even presented examples that spoke to me from the realm of science fiction that I knew about, from *Star Trek* to *The Matrix*. I really recommend that you take this course if you want to expand your intellectual horizons and you have not already been introduced to the study of philosophy. My objective here is to just present an overview of the world of philosophy in the context of my spiritual journey. I hope that any philosophers who might read this go easy on me, because I'm just an ordinary layman on the subject, and I'm sure they will see errors in my thought processes as I present them here. Remember, it's just me trying to make sense of my world. That's all.

Shall we begin?

The actual meaning of philosophy is "love of wisdom," and the goal of the study of philosophy is simply knowledge. The philosopher is open to rational inquiry of anything and thinks that nothing should be believed if it does not survive that process. Philosophy is considered the mother of all disciplines. What we now classify as questions of physics, chemistry, biology, math, medicine, economics, ethics, religion, language, politics, or business were once the purview of the philosopher. As the early philosophers discovered the truths they were looking for, their discoveries spawned these new disciplines. Before the foundations of the sciences were spelled out, sciences were called natural philosophy because questions were asked about our natural world. As the answers came to the early philosophers, the sciences emerged out of the realm of philosophy.

Every person has opinions, intuitions, and gut feelings on a range of subjects, but the philosopher must be able to put these feelings aside and subject these beliefs to tests of validity. In short, the philosopher must value intellectual honesty in the quest for truth in order to gain knowledge. The philosopher must reason, but he must reason carefully. He can't let his preconceived ideas, prejudices, opinions, and gut feelings rule his thoughts.

But how do we reason carefully?

Fortunately, the philosophers have some time-tested tools of logic that can help them reason wisely.

First, there is deductive logic, where the argument moves from general to specific in the search of truth. For example:

All men are mortal.

Socrates is a man.

Therefore, Socrates is mortal.

The truth of the argument is guaranteed by the truth of the premises. If the premises are true, then it would not be possible for the conclusion to be false.

Secondly, there is inductive logic, where the reasoning often goes from the specific to the universal. Please note that the premises of an inductive argument **aren't supposed to guarantee** the conclusion. They are merely supposed to provide good support to the conclusion.

Let's look at a couple of examples.

There is a form of enumerative induction called polling, where a sample of answers from a population is taken to infer or draw a conclusion about what the entire population would answer. This method isn't foolproof and does not lead to exact answers, but it gets you closer to the truth.

Another form would be an argument from analogy. For example: Mice possess a genome similar to man. Therefore, if a medicine affects mice in a certain way, then it is reasonable to expect that the medicine will affect man in the same way.

Again, I think it is important to state that inductive logic is not going to guarantee that you will reach the truth of the matter. It just helps you on the way to that truth, but with the warning: Beware; the conclusion could possibly be wrong. As long as you are skeptical, you should be alright.

Another form of reasoning the philosopher has at his disposal is abductive reasoning. This form of reasoning also comes with the same warning: Be skeptical, because it doesn't necessarily guarantee the truth of the hypothesis. However, this reasoning still gets you closer to the truth, and this is the form of reasoning that has provided major advances in scientific knowledge.

Abductive reasoning uses five criteria to put a hypothesis to the test. They are: testability, fruitfulness, scope, simplicity, and conservatism. Let's talk a little bit about each.

Testability: To test a hypothesis, you predict what you would expect to observe if that hypothesis were true in certain conditions, then see if that prediction comes true in those conditions.

Fruitfulness: When a hypothesis is testable, it makes observable, novel predictions. But when a hypothesis is fruitful, it gets those predictions right.

Scope: The scope of a hypothesis is its explanatory power—that is, how many diverse phenomena the hypothesis explains and how much it unifies our knowledge. The more a hypothesis explains, the more reason we have to think it's true.

Simplicity: A simple explanation, in the scientific sense, does not mean that it is easy to understand. It means that the hypothesis does not invoke more assumptions, entities, or forces than necessary.

Conservatism: In science, when something is conservative, it simply coheres with what we already know; it doesn't contradict already established knowledge.... That is not to say that we should always disregard a hypothesis if it contradicts what we already know. If we always did that, knowledge could never progress. However, if a hypothesis does contradict already established knowledge, that is a strike against it. Unless it can overcome this handicap by being the most fruitful, wide-scoping, and simple hypothesis when compared to the conservative alternatives, it likely should be disregarded. A case in point: It would seem that Einstein's thoughts about light bending around massive objects were not conservative, versus Newton's theory that light always travels in a straight line, but it was determined to be the most fruitful, wide-scoping and simple theory, because it was found that Einstein was right. Light actually does bend around massive objects, and Newton's theory was eventually replaced by Einstein's theory as the best explanation.

Please be aware that this is a very simple explanation for abductive reasoning as I understood it from the course guide, and it really doesn't even start to cover the complexities of how to properly use it to reason correctly. However, my purpose here is to just introduce you to the concept of this form of reasoning, so that you get a sense of this piece of the philosopher's tool kit.

There you have it. Deduction, induction, and abduction are tools that the philosopher has at his disposal. These tools don't guarantee that the philosopher will reach the truth, but they sure help him on his journey.

So, what is truth? There are various theories of truth, but for us laymen or ordinary men, we can simply state that truth is "correspondence to the way the world is" in our quest to gain knowledge, where knowledge can be defined as "justified true belief." I'll try and put it another way. To have knowledge of the way the world really is, we then should be able to justify our thoughts by some sort of tests as already described. I'm sure some philosophers would not agree with my oversimplification here of the terms, but it is a good way for this ordinary man to make sense of my world.

However, true knowledge can be very elusive. For example, in my high school physics classes we learned about Newton's theories of the universe as they relate to gravity. Newton's laws of gravity were able to make correct predictions about the planetary movements. At that time, I believed them as absolute truths. However, Albert Einstein's theory of relativity turned that knowledge on its head. More about the theory of relativity later, but for now, scientists discovered that Newton was incorrect sometimes, because his laws occasionally got the predictions wrong. Please note that science is self-correcting when it gets something wrong; science ensures that other scientists will eventually identify the mistake and correct it.

So, there you have it. The truth can be very elusive. Something you might believe as absolute fact may be disproved at some point in the future. So, what to do? Well, I think that all you can do is to believe what you believe, and just be prepared that your world could be rocked at any time. Ultimately, we might not ever really know the truth. Remember that the Daoists explained through the Daodejing that there are two aspects of Dao, or the way of nature: one that can be talked about and one that cannot be talked about. This belief makes the understanding of the way of nature very limited to humans. So it seems the Daoists understood that man's ability to know the truth is elusive. Please also recall that from Jainism, the Jains understood that there were limitations to human knowledge. They believed in the principle of "non-absolutism," which means that we could be wrong about what we hold as true. Lastly, in the Baha'i faith it is said that humans cannot completely know God because God is greater than the whole, and therefore we will not know the complete truth.

So, is real knowledge possible? I believe the best way to approach life in this respect is to always be open minded. Don't believe everything that you hear or see, even if it comes from experts. Be skeptical.

In ancient Greece, Socrates was considered the wisest man, but he claimed that he really knew nothing. Often, other men would go to Socrates and claim that they knew what something was, but Socrates was able to disprove their knowledge.

Earlier we saw that knowledge was defined as justified true belief, but what if some of the evidence we used for justification was false? When I was younger, I believed Newton's laws of gravity without question, but later saw that Einstein was able to further clarify the laws of gravity.

A similar argument can be said about religious testimony. The Christians believe that "Jesus is God," but if you ask a Muslim, Buddhist, Hindu, Daoist, etc. I am sure that you would find that they will not agree with that statement. Also, you would find that each religion has their own concept of what God is, if they actually believe in a god or gods. They would probably cite certain experiences and testimonies from their religion that points to or justifies in their minds their concept of God and their rituals, but remember, this is only testimony and not proof. Should we believe what they say? That is the question. Another thing to consider is that each religion presents different concepts of their god or gods. How can they all be right? Do we just choose one and hope for the best? No, we need to be skeptical. If there is no proof and only personal testimony, we need to accept that perhaps they could be wrong. If you are a religious person, then that possibility may be very scary for you. So, what should you do? Well, perhaps as I said earlier, maybe you should just believe what you believe until it is disproved, because just remember, even though there is no proof of the religious testimonies, the opposite is also true. For the most part, there is nothing that disproves those testimonies either.

Another case in point are people who experience a miracle. The person experiencing the miracle definitely feels that the experience is real, but should we believe their testimony?

Let's look at a couple of religious figures that had miraculous experiences. In the Christian faith, Saint Paul, while walking alone, saw bright lights and had a vision of Jesus after his death. Jesus was asking him why he was persecuting his followers. This experience resulted in Saint Paul's conversion to Christianity.

In the religion of Islam, Muhammad had similar experiences when he was up on the mountain. He heard God communicating with him and advising him, and this experience ultimately led to the formation of the Islamic religion.

We can choose to believe what each of them said about their miracles, or we can be skeptical. However, there may be another explanation from the realm of science. What Saint Paul and Muhammad experienced may have been temporal lobe epileptic seizures, where they experienced bright lights and heard voices. Of course, there is no proof, because both have been deceased for many centuries and could not be tested by the scientific processes that we have today to determine if someone has temporal lobe epilepsy, but let's imagine for a minute that the technology existed back then to test for this epilepsy. What would we have found? Let's suppose that it was found that they both had temporal lobe epilepsy. Would people at that time have believed their testimony, knowing that science provided a grain of doubt? Perhaps if there was enough doubt, the religions of Christianity and Islam might not have materialized, or at least not in the forms that we know of them today.

We need to be very careful about testimony. If it can't be verified, then perhaps we should move on... or maybe not.

Religions over the centuries have preached to the masses about what to believe. However, there is very little proof to justify their beliefs. In philosophy, faith is a certain kind of belief—belief without sufficient reason of justification. So, why would the masses believe in these religions if there is doubt about the truth being expressed? I think it can be summed up by saying that people in general fear what they don't know, because even though what is being preached can't absolutely be proved, there is a small door ajar in these religions that some, or maybe all, these beliefs may be true. This small door ajar provides hope for people, which is just enough for them to believe. It is a part of human nature to find hope for the things they fear or don't understand. It provides comfort and a sense of mental calm that their world is in order. Isn't that the important thing?

Now let's move on to the really big question: God. God is at the center of most of the world religions in some form or other. A customary way of explaining that God exists is to demonstrate that God's existence is the best explanation for the universe. There appear to be many schools of thought on this matter, but there are many questions. Was the universe created, or did the universe always exist without regard to the passage of time? If it was created, then who or what created it? If the universe always existed, then perhaps there isn't a God, because God wouldn't have been necessary for the universe's creation. Since the universe supports life and there is a certain order required for life to exist, then there must be a God or some sort of intelligent design that allows life to exist as we know it. Or perhaps, can the universe itself be God?

Many philosophers and wise men over the ages have had these thoughts and questions, but it still remains that God's existence can't be proved. The real question is: Is that okay with you? If you are a religious person, then will you let God's existence stand on your faith alone?

Let's take a step in another direction now. Instead of talking about the universal, let's get personal. What does philosophy say about our souls, our free will, and our minds? Most people believe that our souls drive our decisions, giving us the free will to make choices, but from the study of philosophy, they tell us that this is an illusion. Philosophers point out the case of Phineas Gage as an example. Phineas Gage was an even-tempered railroad worker in the 1800s. He had an accident that severely damaged his forebrain. This accident completely changed his personality and his actions. He was no longer even-tempered. He acted completely different after the accident. This case provided serious doubt about our soul's existence and our ability to make free choices in life. If we believe in the soul, we would think that since Phineas' actions were driven by his soul, then things would not have changed. However, this was not the case. He was a completely different man, almost as if he had a different soul. How could this be the case? Well, science has helped to provide some answers. It was soon realized that everyone's personality is not housed in our souls, but in our physical brains. Scientists discovered that everyone's visual activity was housed in the back of the brain, in a place now called the visual cortex. Emotions are the result of brain activity in the limbic system, and decisions are made by the prefrontal cortex, as a few examples. Therefore, if the soul and our free will do not exist, then what can we say about the mind, which is different from the physical brain? It appears that the mind may not exist, either. I commonly think of the mind as "housing" our souls and controlling our decisions. If the soul doesn't exist, then is there a need for a mind? It appears that our physical brains can do what we commonly think the mind does.

Well, here we are. So then, our souls, free will, and minds don't exist? Are they all illusions caused by the physical, electrical impulses and chemical activities of our brain matter, based on inputs received from the environment that we live in? This is a very big pill to swallow. If so, it appears that we are reduced to nothing more than super robots that are programmed to respond to what is happening all around us and then responding in appropriate ways as dictated by our physical brains.

If true, this will clearly shock many people. Most of us feel that we control our destiny by something outside of our physical selves. Take some time and let this realization sink in. There appears to be no hard proof one way or the other in this argument. We will come back to this matter a bit later, as well.

Now, please recall from Robert Wright's book *The Evolution of God* that he presents a case that most humans want to live a comfortable and safe life and that many people will migrate to decisions about their lives and religions that provide this sense of relief and that the way to usually achieve it is through cooperation with others in their environment. Basically, we are responding to our environment in a way to achieve this goal. This is analogous at our personal level where our brains are responding to what it "sees" and then making decisions in our best interest. Could it be that for the most part our brains are programmed to lean toward a social environment that is non-zero sum? It's a thought, but I don't think so. The fact that humans have waged war over the ages doesn't lend support to this argument. I guess you could say that all brains and people don't respond to their environmental inputs in the same way, perhaps because all brains and their brain matter are different. Some brains may be undamaged, some may have been damaged by an accident, some brains may be genetically malformed, some brains may be superior to others in some way, etc. Therefore, I think you cannot make broad assumptions about people's social behavior and how their brains will react to the inputs they receive from their environmental influences. I believe this is just a fact of life.

CHAPTER 7

PHILOSOPHY OF MIND: BRAINS, CONSCIOUSNESS, AND THINKING MACHINES

After finishing the last course on philosophy, I took another Great Course on philosophy. It was Philosophy of Mind: Brains, Consciousness, and Thinking Machines taught by Patrick Grim B. Phil., Ph.D. of the State University of New York at Stony Brook. I was a bit curious about what he had to say on this subject of the mind, because I left the discussion of the mind hanging a bit in the last section.

In this course it explains that Functionalism is the dominant position in the philosophy of mind currently, where Functionalism is the view that mental states are functional states of an organism. "As a functional state, a mental state is triggered by a particular input that (a) results in particular behaviors, but (b) also triggers further mental states down the line." This sounds a lot like what was mentioned earlier where it appears that our brains control our lives, and not our souls, free will, or minds. Even though Functionalism is the dominant position currently in the philosophy of mind, we need to be aware that not all philosophers necessarily agree with it. However, we will use it as the current point of reference.

For now let us assume that our souls, free will, and minds don't exist. If that is the case, then when organisms want or need to perform certain functions, they base their actions on the inputs they receive, which cause changes in their brains which result in their output actions. Could it be that as mentioned previously, humans are nothing more than "super robots"? The current philosophical position of Functionalism seems to lend some support to that idea. In any event, do you believe in the existence of the soul, free will, and the mind? It may be a bit premature to ask that question now, but keep it in the back of your mind – no pun intended. Ultimately, you will have to decide for yourself, because there is no evidence one way or the other.

I also realize that I may have gone beyond the scope of my presentation on religion, God, and spirituality, but have I really? I think that the subject of the soul, free will, and the mind is essential to the understanding of our place in the universe. At least it provides you with a new perspective when you look at your spirituality. Don't you agree?

Let's go a step beyond and bend our minds a bit further on a very interesting subject. This course also speculated about the role of robots in the future of mankind. Today, science is making great strides in the development of robots in the area of artificial intelligence (AI). There are robots that are no longer just programmed to perform certain repetitive tasks such as assembling a car on a factory floor or vacuuming your floors while you are away. Scientists are now starting to program robots to "learn" about their environment and to react to it from what they "see." This sounds a lot like what we humans do every day. This is amazing and raises the question: Will robots someday get better at it then us humans, and if so what will happen? MIT graduate, inventor, and theorist Ray Kurzweil poses this question as the "coming singularity" where robots will be smarter and more efficient than we are and create their own offspring where each generation is improved upon. If or when this ever happens, then what will happen to the human race? Do we sit back and allow this to happen? Or, has the singularity already started down the road? Well, I'm old and probably won't see where this will go, but what about our children and their children? Should they be concerned? Should robotic engineers be restricted in what they should do? I don't know how to answer those questions, but I am sure our children will have to address them in the near future.

However, I am connected to this issue in a personal way. My son-in-law, Mike Carbin, is an assistant professor of computer science at MIT in its CSAIL lab. He and his associates are looking at a way to make artificial intelligence better and faster. Mike and a PhD student, Jonathan Frankle, wrote a paper that was recognized recently by *Popular Mechanics* magazine. The press mentions the following: "MIT researchers have identified a new method to engineer neural networks in a way that allows them to be a tenth of the size of current networks without losing any computational ability, reports Avery Thompson for *Popular Mechanics*. 'The breakthrough could allow other researchers to build AI that are smaller, faster, and just as smart as those that exist today,' Thompson explains. – *Popular Mechanics*"

There you have it! Brilliant people are well on their way to making very smart robots. I just hope that every once in a while they stop and think about the implications to mankind over the coming years and perhaps centuries of development in this area.

But let's look at this issue from another point of view – that of the robots themselves. If this singularity does ever occur, do robots have the same rights as humans to live, breed, and do what they want to do? These are just some of the important questions our descendants may have to answer. A very interesting and potentially scary time to live may be coming, but don't go out and buy that survivalist gear and build a bunker yet. There are people that feel that this singularity could not happen.

So far, computer "brains" are much different from human "brains." Today's computers operate as fully digital. Inputs and outputs are digital, using switches in a very simple form of turning the switches either "on" or "off," with the programming behind it to take advantage of this simple functionality. This may be an oversimplification, but it gives you the general idea at a high level. Human brains are much more complex. The neurons in our brains receive analog inputs and then provide outputs as digital. As an example, a dimmer on a light switch can change the intensity of the light's brightness. This is an example of an analog input. You can then imagine that this dimmer can be an input to a program that measures the intensity, and if it reaches a certain level, it will produce a charge that is then used elsewhere digitally. Again, this is oversimplified, but it should give you the sense that the brain's neurons are more complex. Right now, the human brain can do things that most computers can't do. Our brains can distinguish very subtle inputs and react to them in a way that most computers can't do efficiently. For example, think of recognizing voice inflections and their intentions, or subtle body movements and their intentions. However, they are starting to develop computers to do things like those examples. One example is facial recognition, but it appears that there still are very many challenges ahead for artificial intelligence. Anyway, we don't know if there will be a time when robots will be smarter and more efficient than humans, but it looks like there is certainly a possibility that day could arrive at some point in the future.

So where are we now in this study of philosophy? We have explored quite a bit about what there is to be said about what I call the "pure" philosophy, which is the quest for wisdom, knowledge, and truth in the universe as a whole. Now let's move on to a more specific philosophy – the philosophy of religion – and see what that can tell us about religion, God, and spirituality.

Chapter 8

PHILOSOPHY OF RELIGION

To understand more about the philosophy of religion, I took the Great Course by that title at the end of 2017. It was taught by Professor James Hall from the University of Richmond. He points out right away that examining religion philosophically is a tricky business because there are many different religions in the world, and people also have different concepts of what religion amounts to. Previously, I pointed out my observation, from looking at religions critically so far, that I believed that just about everyone "tailors" their religious beliefs to their own end in one fashion or another. I don't think that there are many people who believe the various doctrines and dogmas of their chosen religion as they are written and preached exactly as stated. I believe people tailor their beliefs about God and their religion in a way that will make them feel the most comfortable. Professor Hall probably didn't mean that exactly, but that is my belief.

He also mentions that people have different ideas as to what philosophy means. In our journey through these courses so far on the subject of philosophy, we discovered that it is the search for wisdom, knowledge, and truth. Prior to taking any of these Great Courses, my best definition for philosophy would have been simply what someone believed about a subject, or more simply, their "beliefs" on the matter. I guess it depends on the circumstances at hand at any given time as to how you should interpret its meaning.

Let's get started. Professor Hall states that our central questions are:

1) "Can humans know whether the claim 'God exists' is true or not?"
2) "If so, how?"
3) "If not, why not?"

An important point to make here is that most people when they start a course on philosophy of religion probably really want to know simply "Does God exist?" I know that was my focus when I started this whole endeavor years ago. However, Professor Hall implies that even though that is the central question, what needs to be done is to focus on the method of examination of God and religion, and that is what he does. Right up front, it needs to be stated that in his course he focused entirely on "ethical monotheism" which is the belief that there is just one God that exists that is all powerful, all knowing and all good. He narrows this study down because otherwise the course would be much too long, and also because most of his audience for this course would be ethical monotheists such as Christians, Jews, or Muslims.

Let's look at the meaning of philosophy of religion. It is not a study of rational arguments or "apologetics" in defense of a faith or faiths. It is not comparative religion. It is not psychology of religion. It is not a history of religion. It is not theology or the study of the nature of God or religious beliefs. It is not religious philosophy, which is done from a religious point of view or belief. It is simply philosophy of religion, which examines religion from a philosophical point of view, trying to gain wisdom, truth, and knowledge. In order to start on this journey of examination, we need to define what is meant by "God." Professor Hall states: " 'God' designates some force, entity, being, or process that is affirmed as a proper object of human worship." This is the generally accepted definition of God, and this is the definition that he uses throughout the course, where he further narrows down the scope of "God" to the ethical monotheist definition I stated above, for practical reasons.

There are three kinds of arguments for the existence of God that Professor Hall provided: the ontological, the cosmological, and the teleological arguments.

The ontological argument is hard for me to grasp completely, and rather than trying to explain it fully where I may make some false statements, I recommend that you do a little research yourself on it. However, I will state that it is an argument used by philosphers from the past, such as Saint Anselm and Rene Descartes. In my simple mind, the ontological argument simply uses reasoning to "prove" that God exists. It uses no evidence that I can tell – just thought and reasoning. To me it is almost like "willing" God into existence. Also, I think that probably most modern-day philosophers do not give much credibility to this argument.

The cosmological and teleological arguments are much easier to understand, because they use human experience based on what is happening in the world and the universe, and applying reasoning to this experience to come to conclusions about God.

The cosmological argument is an argument of "sufficient reason." It states that every event has a cause. For example, a burned-down house could have had a cause where the fire in the fireplace was unattended and a spark ignited the curtain to the window near the fireplace. When we look at this type of argument, we can see how all the events in the world are caused by some other event previous to it. So, one can trace back cause by cause and see that everything that happened in the universe was caused by something else, at least until you start to realize and ask: Was there a first cause? If so, could that have been caused by God? Many people believe that this is true, but again, there is no proof. However, let's pose a question. What if there were no first cause and that the cause and event cycle goes back in time and is never-ending infinitely? That thought certainly throws up some doubt about God as the originator of the events of the world. Another thing to consider for the ethical monotheists is that not all events caused are good for humankind. Some examples are: tornadoes, hurricanes, Ebola, earthquakes, etc. It leads to the question: If God is all good, then why do these terrible things happen? In any event, in my opinion the Cosmological argument doesn't seem to hold much weight.

The teleological argument is also an argument of "sufficient reason." It argues that there is evidence of God's design apparent in nature itself, and it recognizes God's intention of designing the world and the universe in this way. If you look around, you can see evidence of a grand design. Just look at the sunrise or sunset on a beautiful summer day, viewing the northern lights if you are lucky enough to live in northern latitudes, the wonderful design of scallop shells lying in the sand, etc. I'm sure you can give me many more examples as well. You must also consider miracles and divine encounters that are reported as evidence of God's touch. However, one must be careful. Miracles and divine encounters are open to interpretation by the one experiencing the event. Should we always take their word for their experience? Earlier, I mentioned the visions of Saint Paul and Muhammad as possibly a temporal lobe epileptic seizure where they experienced bright lights and heard voices. This doesn't mean that they did not hear or see God. It just throws some doubt as to whether their experience is proof that they actually had an encounter with God. One can see that you have to take every reported miracle or divine encounter with a "grain of salt." However, if you are the one that experiences the miracle, it might be very hard to do this, because in your view it is actually real, as far as you are concerned, so you cannot blame Saint Paul and Muhammad for believing their experiences with God.

Let's get back to the wonders of the beautiful design we see all around us as evidence of God's handiwork. Yes, we see the beautiful clouds on a sunny day, the colorful and pretty flowers in our garden, the hummingbirds pollinating the flowers, and the stately hawks in the air looking for their next meal, but we see all too many ordinary things as well that are not quite as impressive such as misshapen rocks in the yards, weeds overgrowing some of the flowers, and vines strangling some trees in the marshlands. Are these part of God's design and intention as well? Yes, they are. You could say that "beauty is in the eye of the beholder."

Another thing to consider as it relates to God's design and intention is the bad things that happen in the world, such as tornadoes, hurricanes, Ebola, earthquakes, etc. Also, what about the bad things that people do to each other or the environment? Some things are unintentional, but then there are people like Hitler and Osama Bin Laden who intentionally did bad things to people. It raises the question: Why would God design and intend that these things to occur? If there is a God, then perhaps he is not all good as we defined earlier, or perhaps he is all good but there is another God-like being that causes this evil. Well, there is no proof either way, and there is no proof so far that God exists either as we have seen in our studies so far. Therefore, I believe I should take the teleological argument with a "grain of salt" as well.

In any event, there are theists that present arguments aimed at reconciling divine existence with the apparent evils in the world. These arguments are called theodicies. One justification of the theists is that even with evil present in the world, it still is the best of all possible worlds. However, I'm not sure I buy that argument. Another way that theists provide justification is to state simply that God is not responsible for the bad things. Perhaps evil is the result of the bad things that humans do and God is providing punishment to get them back in line with his wishes. As pointed out above, there is also an argument that there is another "God-like" being that is the opposite of God that is causing all the mayhem in the world. In the Christian faith, we would call that being the devil. There is also another thought that evil exists in the world so that man can rise above it and do good deeds in spite of everything around it so that these good deeds can glorify God. The book of Job in the Old Testament of the Christian Bible comes to mind for me here. However, this raises the question that we have presented earlier about whether man has free will. Perhaps he does, or perhaps he doesn't, and everything man does is a response to the events occurring in his environment based on the chemical, electrical, and mechanical reactions in the brain of man and has nothing to do with free will. Well, you will have to think about that and come to a decision on your own.

I applaud the theists for trying to justify the existence of God by presenting these arguments or opinions, but this is still not a proof of God's existence. So, where do we go now? What should the faithful do now? Professor Hall basically uses the remaining lectures to show why the faithful actually believe what they believe. He spends a lot of time talking about paradigms. A paradigm, as used here, is simply a way to view the world. One example is that many people believe that humans could never understand God because God is beyond human comprehension. However, the various religions build or have built their own views of the world and frame this view in a way that makes them feel comfortable with their beliefs about God. Proof that God exists is not relevant to their faiths. They simply take "a leap of faith" and frame their world around this leap of faith. Since they are completely invested in their world view, it would be hard for them to see another point of view. This view of the world may or may not be the way the world actually is, but to them, it doesn't matter. They are comfortable with how they see it. Living in a certain paradigm can have ill effects for those who don't subscribe to those beliefs. For example, a country that believes in a certain view of the world could order that all people, regardless of their beliefs, subscribe to their religious laws. This can be dangerous if those laws infringe on the rights of others with a different view of their lives. I'm sure you can think of a few examples in the world today where that might happen or is happening presently.

Lastly, before I close out this discussion on the philosophy of religion, I just want to state that even though there is no proof that a god or gods exist, there is also no proof that they don't. If you are religious, you just have to make that leap and believe whatever you feel comfortable with, in the framework of your own spiritual and religious beliefs. As an observation, I believe that most all religions are good. Most religions provide stories for good moral behavior and seem to teach their people the right way to act and behave in a moral and just society. This is a good thing, and I think that all religions provide a good social fabric for people to get along and live together in peace, whether or not they believe in God, or ultimately whether there is a God or not.

Chapter 9

A Few Comments on Supernatural Occurrences and Miracles

few of you are probably looking at the title for this section and thinking, "Is Jim going off the rails? He has presented fairly well-researched and accurate information up to this point, and now is he going to present these occurrences and miracles as fact without evidence or proof?" Well, no. However, to many people in the world, these occurrences and miracles are very important to their religious and spiritual beliefs, so I need to provide a little background on the subject.

Many people believe in ghosts, people with special powers and abilities, miracles, aliens, etc. I am not going to address each specifically because I think that they all fall into a category we could call "unexplained occurrences." Since this work is about religion, God, and spirituality, I will choose to focus on a specific religious miracle. In looking at miracles on the internet, I disregarded a number of them right away. I wanted to find one that had a feeling of credibility to it. I found one. Yes, it is from a religious website, but before passing judgment, please read it. Before starting, you need to note that in the Christian religions, a host is piece of bread that represents the body of Christ, and which is eaten during the worship service in order to obtain the goodness of Christ.

The below can be found at: visionsofjesuschrist.com/weeping2124.html

'In October of 2008, an extraordinary event took place at St. Anthony of Padua parish church in Sokółka, Poland. A consecrated Host was transformed into a fragment of muscle tissue belonging to a living human heart suffering severe stress and on the point of death.

Transformation of the Host

At 8:30, on Sunday morning October 12, 2008, Fr. Filip Zdrodowski was celebrating Holy Mass at the above-mentioned church. While Fr. Jacek Ingielewicz was assisting him in distributing Holy Communion, one of the hosts fell by accident on the altar step. A woman parishioner kneeling nearby noticed it and pointed it out to Fr. Jacek who promptly picked it up. Observing that the Host was soiled, he placed it in the vasculum, a small bowl of water standing beside the tabernacle (the vasculum is the little basin the priest washes his fingers in after distributing Holy Communion).

After the Mass, the scranton, Sister Julia Dubowska, took the vasculum into the sacristy, emptied its contents into another vessel, and locked it away in the safe. Only she and the pastor, Msgr.

Stanisław Gniedziejko, had a key to the safe. It is worth noting that Sr. Julia is a member of the Congregation of the Sisters Servants of Jesus in the Eucharist whose special charism is to promote veneration of Jesus present in the Blessed Sacrament.

Having never before dealt with such a situation, Sr. Julia examined the vessel every day to see if the consecrated Host had dissolved. Normally the host dissolves completely in the water after several days. She expected the same to occur in this case. On October 19, around eight o'clock in the morning, upon opening the sacristy safe, Sr. Julia recognized the smell of bread. She assumed that the Host had dissolved completely and that she could now empty the contents of the vasculum into the sacrarium, a special drain located near the altar.

When she looked at the Host in the vessel she was struck dumb with amazement. In the center of the white Host she saw what looked like a bloody piece of living flesh measuring about a centimeter by a centimeter and a half. As laboratory analysis would later show, it was real muscle tissue characteristic of a living human heart in the agony of death, as if on the point of cardiac arrest. Sr. Julia stared at the extraordinary object with the greatest astonishment and reverence. She confessed that she felt like Moses gazing on the bush in the wilderness that burned without being consumed.

Seeing the nun standing motionless so long over the transformed Host, Fr. Filip Zdrodowski asked her what was the matter. Sr. Julia explained to him what she had in her hand and how the consecrated Host came to be there. She placed the vessel on the desk so that the Monsignor and the other priests present in the sacristy might see the transformed Host.

Msgr. Stanisław Gniedziejko would later recall his shock at seeing the blood-red substance on the white Host. The water in which it was immersed remained untinged by the blood. On taking a closer look at the bloody substance on the Host, he saw something resembling a piece of flesh—a bloody fragment of living tissue. Everyone knew this was a consecrated Host in which the Risen Christ was present in His glorified human nature. They began to wonder if this red substance on the Host were the result of a natural process, or if it might not be a supernatural sign through which Christ wished to make something very important known. The Monsignor immediately cautioned those present against trivializing the mysterious phenomenon. That same day he informed His Excellency Archbishop Edward Ozorowski of the incident. Shortly afterwards, the Archbishop paid a visit to Sokółka. On examining the Host, he gave orders that it should be kept safe and observed closely.

On October 29, the vessel containing the Host was transferred to the tabernacle of the Divine Mercy Chapel in the parish presbytery. The following day, the Archbishop had the Host removed from the water, placed on a white corporal, enclosed in a pyx, and deposited in the tabernacle. In a short while, the Host dried out. The reddish brown bloody substance encrusted itself onto the corporal, and thus it remains to this day. For three years the Host was kept in the presbytery chapel. Not until October 2, 2011 was it solemnly brought back to the church and displayed for daily adoration in the chapel of Our Lady of the Rosary....

The expertise of two outstanding scientists

On August 5, 2009, on the Archbishop's instructions, the Metropolitan Curia of Białystok sent a letter to Profs. Maria

Sobaniec-Łotowska and Stanisław Sulkowski of the Białystok Medical University requesting their scientific expertise on "the material adhering to the Host as preserved at St. Anthony of Padua parish church in Sokółka." The letter stressed the need for treating the matter "with all due seriousness, urgency, and in the strictest confidence." Profs. Maria Sobaniec-Łotowska and Stanisław Sulkowski are both outstanding scientists, highly respected in Poland and abroad. For thirty years they have specialized in the field of histopathological diagnostics and have many academic achievements to their credit. They work in two separate branches of the Białystok Medical University: the Institute of Medical Pathomorphology and the Institute of General Pathomorphology.

On August 7, 2009, Prof. Maria Sobaniec-Łotowska traveled to Sokółka where, in the presence of a special commission, she took a sample of the mysterious substance on the Host. "When I took the sample," she states, "I had no idea what this substance was. I obtained a small amount of it. It was brown in color and adhered closely to the preserved fragment of the Blessed Host. " The two professors conducted separate, rigorously scientific analyses of the sample of the Host. Using state-of-the-art light and electron microscopes, they photographed and made detailed descriptions of the morphological images.

The results of the separate, independent analyses were in complete agreement with each other, greatly astonishing the two scientists. It turned out that the mysterious substance into which the fragment of the Host had changed was muscle tissue of a human heart experiencing the agony of death—as if on the point of cardiac arrest. Professor Maria Sobaniec-Łotowska explains: "In the tiny fragment of material, which we examined, we found the presence of several morphologically distinctive markers indicating myocardial tissue. One of these markers is the phenomenon of segmentation, i.e. damage to heart muscle fibers at the zone of insertion, and the phenomenon of fragmentation. These lesions appear as multiple small cracks, as if cut with a knife. Such changes occur only in necrotic fibers and reflect the rapid contractions of the heart muscle in the final stages of death.

Another important proof that the test material comes from the muscle of a human heart is the mainly centralized configuration of the nuclei in the observed fibers, which is characteristic of that muscle. Along the length of some of the fibers we also found patterns consistent with node contractions. Closer electron-microscopic examination revealed outlines of the insertion points and delicate microfibrillar networks. Summarizing our findings in the report to the Archdiocesan Curia, we stated: ' The material (...) indicates myocardial tissue, or at least, of all the tissues of a living body, it most resembles it. ' And what is important, in our opinion, is the fact that the material we analyzed consists entirely of this tissue. " Professor Stanisław Sulkowski emphasizes, "The matter comprising the Host quickly dissolves when immersed in water. But the Blessed Host from Sokółka has not broken down for reasons that remain baffling to science. What is still more remarkable is the fact that the middle portion of the Host turned into heart muscle tissue, forming an inseparable structure with the rest of the white Host."

The photomicrographs are empirical, scientific proof that no one could have united the two structures—heart muscle tissue and bread. Even scientists equipped with the most up-to-date equipment could not produce anything like it, so closely is the matter of the Host united and interpenetrated with the heart muscle fibers. This excludes any possibility of human interference. Professor Maria Sobaniec-Łotowska stresses, "This extraordinary and mysterious interpenetration of the white Ghosts material with human heart muscle fibers was observed, examined, and photographed using both light and electron microscopy. The indication is that there could not have been any human intervention. Yet another extraordinary fact bears mentioning. The Host remained immersed in water for a considerable length of time, after which it was placed on the corporal. Yet our studies indicated none of the changes one would have expected of heart muscle fibers being immersed in water for so long a period. From the point of view of empirical research, we are unable to explain this fact. These are undoubtedly the most important studies I have conducted in my life. The results were shocking to me. They point to an extraordinary phenomenon, which from a scientific standpoint, is simply inexplicable. "

The transformation of the consecrated Host into the muscle of a human heart in its death agony is a sign calling us all to repentance. It is a reminder to all of us that every Holy Mass is a re-presentation (making present) of the passion, death and resurrection of Christ and that Christ is truly present in the consecrated Host in His glorified, resurrected humanity, in order that He may offer Himself to us as our "antidote to death...."'

Well, there you have it. This miracle seems to be documented very well. All of the facts are present, and there is detail about the verification of the miracle. As you can see from the last paragraph, the religious of that town in Poland take this matter very seriously and believe that it is in fact an actual supernatural occurrence that is proved as true.

Well, you be the judge. I tend to be skeptical, because I wasn't there at the time, but you have to admit that the priests and scientists who experienced this event cannot be blamed for believing in this miracle, which proves my point. Each and every one of us experiences life in different ways, with different experiences, and we cannot be blamed if we believe in something strongly, whether we experience it directly or are influenced by people we respect. It is called faith, and is a good thing if it makes us feel comfortable with our place in this great universe.

Science

THE SPIRITUAL BRAIN:
SCIENCE AND RELIGIOUS
EXPERIENCE

$\mathcal{N}$ow that we have covered a great deal on the matters of the various worlds of religions and philosophy, I think it is time to move on to science and see what, if anything, it can tell us about God and religions from a completely different perspective. To ease into our discussion, let's look at the brain and its relation to religious and spiritual experiences.

Again, as I have throughout this discussion, I rely on The Great Courses to help provide insight. I took a Great Course called The Spiritual Brain: Science and Religious Experience. It was taught by Dr. Andrew Newberg of the Myrna Brind Center of Integrative Medicine at Thomas Jefferson University Hospital. He is board certified in internal and nuclear medicine, but more importantly for us, he has spent a great deal of time studying religious and spiritual experiences and the effects they have on the brain, and vice-versa.

In the course, he introduced us to the various parts and functions of the brain in detail. I'm not going to go into such depth, because I think I will deviate too much from my objective of trying to be somewhat simple in my explanations; however, I still want to present enough for you to get a general understanding of the miracle of the brain and how it relates to our human nature of finding meaning and insight in and from religious and spiritual experiences.

So, let's get going. Dr. Newberg introduces us to a new area of science called "neurotheology," which is essentially the study of the relationship between the brain and spirituality.

A quote from the course: "The tools of neurotheology are brain imaging techniques and other physiological measures of the brain and body, such as changes in blood pressure, heart rate or immune function. Other tools include studies and experiments that measure subjective experience, including thoughts, feelings and perceptions." Questionnaires are good at getting information on subjective experiences.

In addition to these techniques, the tools of psychology are helpful. The ancient Buddhists and Hindus have long "made extensive evaluations of the experience of the self, our emotional attachment to the self, how the human psyche can be altered through various practices. These traditions recognized the importance of using the brain to help us achieve spiritual enlightenment."

One must also consider the importance of the evolutionary development of the brain. The brain must have adapted over time to survive, because the world is a cruel place to live, with all sorts of "beings" competing for food sources and power. So, if the brain can adapt to learn how to grow crops and domesticate animals, then it probably can adapt to think about such things as the meaning of life and the powers beyond man, which will most likely lead to contemplation of religious and spiritual questions.

Dr. Newberg spends a lot of time in the course talking about the various parts of the brain, and the various brain functions, in detail. However, I will give only general descriptions here, to keep it as simple as possible. The first system is the autonomic nervous system, which is the system that connects the brain with the body through the body's nerves. There are two parts to this system. The sympathetic nervous system is an arousal system which turns on when there is something in our environment that we really need to pay attention to right away. You could call it the "fight or flight" response. The other part is the parasympathetic nervous system, which is designed to calm us down and rejuvenate our energy stores. These two systems work generally at different times to help us survive in our environment. However, when these two systems are activated at the same time during some religious and spiritual experiences, the religious experience can be very calming and blissful but at the same time it will arouse and alert us to the significance of the experience.

The autonomic nervous system is regulated by the limbic system, which can be thought of as the primary emotional controller of the brain. One can see that a religious or spiritual experience can be very emotional and involve many different feelings such as awe, reverence, and wonder, which could turn on both parts of the autonomic nervous system and give one the experience mentioned just above.

From a physical standpoint, there are four parts, or lobes, of the brain. The occipital lobe is located in the back of the brain. The frontal lobe is located in the front part of the brain. The temporal lobe is located on the side of the brain, and lastly the parietal lobe is located toward the back top of the brain.

The occipital lobe is associated with what we see. The occipital lobe really only sees things like lines, shapes, and colors but other areas of the brain, called association areas, construct and connect these into pictures that we recognize.

The frontal lobe can be thought of as the attention area. When we focus our attention on doing a certain task, it is the frontal lobe that is turned on.

The parietal lobe takes all our sensory information and helps us orient ourselves to the world around us. It provides us with a sense of "self."

The main function of the temporal lobe is to process and analyze auditory information. It also plays a role in memory, personality, and behavior.

In addition to what has been mentioned, there are other functions of the brain. The verbal-conceptual function helps us with language, concepts, and abstract ideas and is located between the temporal and parietal lobes. There is a quantitative function that helps us with numbers. There is a binary function that helps us with opposites, such as right versus wrong, which can play a big part in spirituality. There is a causal function, which allows us to recognize causes and effects in the world. There is an existential function that tells us when something is real or not. There is a reductionistic function which breaks things down into parts, and likewise, there is a holistic function that binds or brings things together. There is an abstract area that allows us to think about things even though those thoughts don't have physical or concrete existence. Clearly, you can see how each of these parts and functions could be important in a spiritual or religious experience in some way. However, I just want to point out that these parts and functions are just a few of the many complexities of the brain. If you have further interest or want more detail, I recommend that you take Dr. Newberg's course, because I am only giving you a flavor of what the brain is all about in this discussion, and I hope Dr. Newberg forgives me for oversimplifying what he presented in the course.

In order to study the effects of religious or spiritual activity on the brain, you must narrow down what you want to study and figure out the best method to measure this activity. Dr. Newberg describes a study performed on Franciscan nuns in 1993 at the University of Pennsylvania. They decided to perform brain scans on the nuns while they were performing a specific type of prayer called centering prayer, which is a type of prayer where the participant focuses on a sacred word or phrase for approximately twenty minutes. They also selected nuns who were experienced in this type of prayer for at least fifteen years, to qualify for this testing. They found that during the test, the nuns had increased activity in the prefrontal cortex, which is part of the frontal cortex, and decreased activity in the parietal lobes, amongst other things. This is interesting because it shows that the prefrontal cortex must have been focusing highly on the task at hand of repeating the sacred word or words, while the parietal lobe released the nuns' sense of self or oneness during this activity. This certainly is understandable, because in deep prayer or meditation, even I lose a bit of my connection with the world and my place in it.

Dr Newberg also presented studies or brain scans done on atheists or non-believers doing similar activities of prayer or meditation. It is interesting to note that those scans looked different between the two groups. Perhaps, it is because each group had developed different cognitive ways of thinking about God over their lifetimes up to that point and those thoughts and feelings affected how each of them thought about God and religion based on each of their own personal experiences. In the course, Dr Newberg makes mention of the book, The Stages of Faith, written by James Fowler, which presents the seven stages of spiritual development. From the course, I see these stages simply as the evolution of each individual's brain and mind over a lifetime, but this evolution may result in completely different outcomes in different people based on each individual's experiences in life. For example, a person raised in a loving, caring and religious household that develops and lives a stable and ideal life will probably have a different spiritual outlook then an individual who is abused.

It was also pointed out that different studies have shown that prayer and meditation resulted in physical changes, such as: decreased heart-rate, blood pressure, metabolism, and hormonal changes. Meanwhile, it also increased certain chemicals such as serotonin, dopamine, and GABA while decreasing certain other chemicals such as cortisol and norepinephrine. So it appears that these chemicals in the brain or neurotransmitters which communicate between nerve cells may play a role in why we feel spiritual. Since I'm not a doctor, I am assuming that the respective increase and decrease of these chemicals is a good thing for the human body, as well as the spiritual well-being. If so, it appears that prayer and meditation could have a positive effect on a person's physical and mental health.

Dr. Newberg also discusses the effects of drugs and near-death experiences on the brain. Basically, I think that these experiences raise more questions than they answer about the reality of these experiences. Do the drugs and near-death experiences affect the brain in a positive or negative way in which we perceive reality? Is what we see in these states real, or an altered view of reality? There is no evidence one way or the other, so one must be skeptical. He noted how hard it would be to develop experiments for observing near-death experiences, because quite frankly, no one knows when they will occur. However, he pointed out one technique that could be used to help us understand more about near-death experiences. Since many people that have these experiences report a sense of floating above their bodies to the top of the room, he suggested that emergency and operating rooms place written messages or images of things on the tops of cabinets that could only be seen from the ceiling. Then, if a person has a near-death experience in one of these rooms, researchers could ask these individuals after the experience to tell them if they saw anything on the tops of the cabinets. Can you imagine if someone actually reported accurately what was located on one of these cabinets after a near-death experience? It blows my mind to think about the possibilities from here to imagine not only the powers of the brain and/or mind, but the existence of a soul not attached to the body and all the unanswered questions about what is real and, yes, even the existence of God. But for now, let's come back down to earth.

Dr. Newberg also talks about myths and rituals. From this part of the course, I have come to believe that myths, which are basically stories, are ways that the brain adjusts to the world and universe around it. Whether or not the myths are true, I believe that the brain is reacting to its environment and constantly trying to find answers. If answers cannot be found, then the brain will make up stories to help explain the things it does not know or cannot see. Myths or stories about Moses and the burning bush and the story of Muhammad being raised up to heaven are examples of that, and they help explain in the minds of some men that there is a God, even if there is no proof. Likewise, man has created rituals to help reinforce these myths in the minds of the followers of the various world religions. The repetition, day in and day out or week in and week out, helps the brain keep track of the world and make sense of it. For example, the Christian Catholic Mass reminds us on a weekly basis that Jesus, who is God, died for our sins and was raised up to heaven to provide salvation for us. This mass is repeated so often during a person's lifetime that it would be hard to believe otherwise for a good practicing Catholic.

I guess you could say that myths are beliefs, and a belief can be defined as a "feeling" that something exists or is true even without proof. There is a distinction between what is true and not true based on proof, but here is the catch. What constitutes proof may be and probably is different for science, religion, theology, and philosophy. For example, a priest may say that some or all the Bible stories are proof of God's existence, like when Jesus came down to Paul and asked him why was he persecuting Christians; however, a philosopher would say that this is not proof because there is no historical written evidence from multiple sources that this actually occurred. There is just this Bible story. Belief in this story is based on faith alone, and in some circles I'm sure that would constitute proof. I believe that what I am writing here is as true as it can be, but as you read my words, remember to take what I am saying with a grain of salt, because I could be wrong. I am writing from my research and a lot of good information from many college professors and experts, and I am doing my best to write what I believe is true and correct. I am also writing from my thoughts, memories, and experiences, but we all know that our memories can sometimes fool us into believing something that may not be correct or true.

In this course, Dr. Newberg provides a lot of information on how the physical brain seems to be well adapted to lead us to spiritual thoughts, but if I step back and look at what the brain is really doing, I then see that the brain in each one of us appears to be simply reacting to its environment and developing its way to survive in this sometimes good and sometimes hostile environment called earth.

If our experiences in life are "good," then we may develop positive spiritual beliefs, and if we are abused, we may develop another view of spirituality. Everything is based on our environment and experiences which will lead us to how and what we believe. However, I do agree with Dr. Newberg that the brain is uniquely adapted to be spiritual, and I will take it one step further. The brain in each one of us is unique and the spiritual beliefs we form will only be ours alone, even if our spiritual beliefs are not spiritual at all.

Next, we will continue on our scientific journey with a look at the theory of relativity and quantum mechanics and see if that may shed any light on God and spirituality.

Chapter 11

THEORY OF RELATIVITY AND QUANTUM MECHANICS

$\mathscr{I}$ took the Great Course Einstein's Relativity and the Quantum Revolution: Modern Physics for Non-Scientists, 2nd Edition, taught by Professor Richard Wolfson of Middlebury College. Professor Wolfson did a very good job of making the course material understandable on a subject that really makes you scratch your head while you are trying to grasp the concepts that he presented, but I have to say that quite frequently through this course I had to take what was presented at face value and assume that the many scientists that made the various discoveries were correct in their assumptions and theories. As with the study of philosophy, where one tries to determine the truth of some concept or belief, the truth may be elusive. We just have to assume that what we think is the truth really is the "truth," at least until someone else comes along and presents a better case or argument for the "truth." This appears to be the case with the concepts and theories of modern physics as well, but in this course Professor Wolfson mentions and sometimes shows how these theories appear to be correct based on our observations at this point in time in the history of science. Therefore, we can believe these concepts and theories for now until new discoveries either expand our understanding of modern physics or change them altogether. In my presentation here I will present only what was discovered or theorized. I will not try to teach or show you, because I am grossly underqualified to do that for you. If you really want to understand these concepts and theories, I really recommend that you take this course because Professor Wolfson does a very good job of making a difficult subject somewhat understandable to the layman.

Now, what does the theory of relativity and quantum mechanics or the study of science in general have to do with our subject here of finding out more about God, spirituality, and the various religions of the world? Well, to be frank, I don't know. However, I have a feeling that if we can look at what the universe is showing us through science at least as to how we understand science in the present day we may just possibly get a glimpse into God, if there is a God, or some kind of intelligent design that we could call God. As we have seen, there is no proof that God exists, and quite frankly neither you nor I will ever prove that God exists but it doesn't mean there isn't a God or some intelligent design in our universe. There are a lot of people in the world today who believe God exists. As we have seen, they have faith even without the proof. I also want to believe in God; even though I realize there is no proof, I still want to reach out and explore everything I can to add to my understanding of our existence in this world and universe, whether or not there really is a god or gods. I think science may help me add little pieces to this understanding. I may not find anything in this exploration, but then again I may – so I will try.

When I started this course, I had only a marginal experience or knowledge of this subject matter. While I was in college in the 1970s at Norwich University, only a few miles away from Middlebury College up in Vermont where Professor Wolfson teaches, I did study a bit of physics as part of my mathematics curriculum. However, my studies were limited to classical and/or "Newtonian" physics, and I can't recall that we even touched upon the subject of "modern" physics, so when I took this Great Course it was all pretty much new to me. The course copyright is from the year 2000, but the subject matter in the course is pretty current and really hasn't changed since that time, with the exception being the recent discovery of the Higgs boson particle, which Professor Wolfson indicated may be close to discovery. He was right. It was discovered on July 4th 2012 at CERN's Large Hadron Collider at the Franco-Swiss border near Geneva.

Before describing modern physics, Professor Wolfson presented classical and "Newtonian" physics as it was understood prior to the 20th century. He showed us the discoveries of Galileo and Newton. He pointed out Newton's three laws of motion:

1) That objects move uniformly unless acted upon by outside forces
2) That a given force produces a change in motion
3) For every action there is an equal and opposite reaction

Newton "developed the concept of 'universal gravitation,' suggesting that every object in the universe attracts every other object, with a force that depends on their masses and the distance between them."

From the ideas of Galileo and Newton came the Principle of Galilean Relativity: The laws of motion work exactly the same way for everyone as long as he or she is in uniform motion (no acceleration).

Basically, Newton's laws showed a predictability in the universe where all of its constituents determined what happens to everything. A "clockwork universe," you could say.

In classical physics, there was also the discovery of electricity and magnetism. Static electricity showed that there were positive and negative charges and that opposite charges attract each other and like charges repelled each other. Likewise, magnets showed that they have two different poles or sides, where opposite magnetic poles attract each other and similar poles repel each other. It was discovered that electric fields create magnetic fields and that magnetic fields create electric fields. In the 1860s, James Clerk Maxwell showed that electric fields and magnetic fields created electromagnetic waves that traveled with the speed of light. Hence, he concluded that light was an electromagnetic wave, which made optical science a branch of the study of electromagnetism.

In the 19th century, scientists thought that light traveled through some sort of "medium" or substance which they called "ether," similar to how water waves travel through water. However, a famous experiment called the Michelson-Morley experiment showed that there is no ether. In 1905 Albert Einstein declared that the ether was fiction, and he asserted his principle of special relativity: The laws of physics are the same for all observers in uniform motion. He also asserted that the speed of light would be the same no matter whether you were measuring it—here on earth standing still, or in a spaceship going close to the speed of light. But how could that be, according to his theory!? Well, Einstein indicated that every observer's concept of space and time could or would be different based on their own personal observation platform. If someone was moving close to the speed of light relative to someone standing on earth, then time would slow down. They wouldn't know it until they returned back to earth and found that they had aged only a little bit and their friends had aged by a number of years. Hence, the term "relative" in this theory. Time is relative to each observer…this "stretching" of time for the observer in the space ship is a time dilation as compared to the observer on earth. This time dilation was shown to be true. In the 1950s, an experiment at Mount

Washington in New Hampshire here in New England showed this to be the case. It was an experiment measuring radioactive subatomic particles, called muons, produced in the earth's upper atmosphere. They travel down to the earth's surface at a speed of .994 of the speed of light—very fast! Scientists were baffled by the fact that quite a few of these muons made it to the surface, because their radioactive decay is so fast that they should have decayed long before hitting the surface. What the scientists found is that the time they traveled to earth from the muons frame of reference was just 1/9 that of the time in the frame of reference at the surface of the earth! That should make you stop and think.

Therefore, events that appear to be simultaneous in one frame of reference may not be simultaneous in another frame of reference. Remember that time on earth is not the same as time on a spaceship traveling close to the speed of light, where time is slowed down. A clock registering 10:10 am on earth as the event in question will not be the same as a clock on the spaceship that might be registering, let's say, 10:00 a.m. instead. From the point of view on the spaceship the event of 10:10 a.m. has not occurred yet. Therefore, we cannot say that the event is simultaneous in both frames of reference.

Here's another mind-bending concept to think about. No one and no object can travel at or above the speed of light. The amount of force required to move or accelerate the object would be infinite, which is certainly not achievable. In 1907, Einstein wrote a paper where he states that $E=mc^2$. This paper shows the equivalence between mass and energy, where "c" is the speed of light. Energy, like mass, manifests itself in inertia which is the resistance that an object has to being moved. You can think of inertia as how hard it is to accelerate an object. The more energy it takes to accelerate an object means the object's inertia is high. As an object is accelerated to a high speed, its inertia also increases. The object becomes harder to accelerate, and the inertia increases without limit as the object's speed approaches the speed of light. Therefore, travel at the speed of light is not possible.

Let's take a step back now and think about E=mc^2. This equation basically states that energy and matter are equivalent by a factor. This has a spiritual dimension, to me. My body has mass, but it really is not just a mass. It is energy as well, in the form of mass. Does this "energy," which is disguised as mass, also have some sort of spiritual connection to the universe? Or better put, is it a part of some sort of intelligent design in our universe?... If so, then I as well as you are part of this intelligent design. Shall we call it "God"? Well, I don't think we can, from an intellectual perspective, because the philosophers would say there is no concrete proof that God exists, but what about from the religious or spiritual perspective? We saw that the religious of the world often don't need concrete proof, because they have faith. Should we have faith, in this case? Let us think about that more and perhaps come back to this question later.

The next topic that Professor Wolfson talks about is gravity. In Newtonian physics, gravity is thought to be some sort of force between objects where this "force" is basically dependent on their sizes and distance from each other. In Newton's theory, he asserts that somehow this force between objects "reaches" out instantaneously to attract each other, but we know that nothing, including a force, can "reach" out faster than the speed of light, at least as far as we know in this time of our scientific history. There will be more on this matter later when we visit the enigma of quantum entanglement, but for now, this problem of gravity presented quite a dilemma.

In 1914, Albert Einstein published a paper which addressed this problem with gravity. Gravity makes objects accelerate toward each other as they get closer to each other, but this is not due to any forces being exerted between these objects. Einstein gave the answer that matter and energy curve space and time or, spacetime, in their vicinity. The more massive an object or energy source is, then the greater the curvature of spacetime. You can think of it in this way as the following simple visual example. Imagine that you spread out a sheet stretched flat in mid-air, tied down on all sides. Now imagine you put a very small pebble in the middle of the sheet, and then you get a very light Styrofoam ball and roll it by the pebble several inches away from it. The Styrofoam ball will probably roll by in a straight line, barely changing direction, if there is any change at all. You can think of the pebble as changing the spacetime "sheet" in its vicinity, but only changing it a little bit because its mass is so small. Now replace the small pebble with a soccer ball. You will now notice that the sheet is bending downward in the vicinity of the soccer ball by quite a bit. Roll your Styrofoam ball by the soccer ball several inches away and now you will notice that the Styrofoam ball curves by the ball as it passes by it, as if the soccer ball is exerting a force on it. Think of this experiment as a visual example of gravity as the spacetime curvature. The more massive the object, the more anything going by it will curve toward it. Additionally, this spacetime "sheet" will produce gravitational waves if the "sheet" is disturbed in some way such as massive objects merging together, like two black holes colliding together. These waves will radiate out at the speed of light. Time should also run slower where gravity or the spacetime curvature is stronger because light loses energy "climbing" away from a very large mass. The speed of light doesn't change, but the frequency of the light waves is reduced. I'll leave it to your research to find the scientific explanation for this phenomenon, but this is what gravity really is, and Einstein called it his theory of general relativity. This theory removes the condition of uniform motion from his theory of special relativity, because in his general theory, gravity accelerates objects in the spacetime continuum. Objects are no longer in uniform motion when they are in the vicinity of each other. This theory also predicts that it curves light when light passes by massive objects like our sun. This has been proved by astronomers. One could say, in summary, that gravity "makes" Einstein's general theory of relativity real to us.

This general theory of relativity also applies nicely to our concept of black holes in space, as I briefly alluded to above. A black hole is an extremely massive object that causes a great curvature in spacetime. It would be like compressing our earth into a ball of one inch in diameter. You can think of a black hole in our "sheet" example as a very big object, such as a bowling ball, replacing the soccer ball in our example; even that would not be massive enough, but we'll use it anyway. As you can imagine, the bending of the sheet will most likely curve our sheet all the way down to the ground, literally creating a "hole" in the vicinity of the bowling ball. Any object rolling by it will actually spiral downward all the way down to the bowling ball itself. I think this gives a pretty good representation of the curvature of spacetime around a black hole. It is said that this curvature is so great that even light cannot escape from it. We've found out above that massive objects can bend light, so it is not hard to believe that a very massive black hole could prevent light from escaping; hence its name. Also, there is a misconception that black holes "suck" things in its vicinity into it, but that is not the case. As an object gets very close to this extreme spacetime curvature it will just spiral down into it, and an infinite amount of energy would be required to escape from this extreme curvature. Additionally, to an outside observer the time dilation would appear that an object entering the object would actually stop, as if time stopped itself. However, to the object entering the black hole, time would still seem to move normally. It is said that super massive black holes are at the center of most galaxies, including our own Milky Way, with the mass of millions or billions of suns and these galactic holes grow as more suns "fall" into these massive black holes. Lastly, scientists speculate that rotating black holes may form "wormholes" which connect remote parts of the spacetime continuum. Well, let's not go there. My head might explode.

Well, there you have it! A very brief and watered-down explanation of Einstein's special and general theories of relativity. You may have to stop and think about this subject a few times, because let's face it! It is not generally intuitive, and it does not seem logical, at least from our everyday observations of how we think the universe really is, but it should make you pause and think. At least I hope so.

Now we move on to the second part of the course, which is quantum physics, or as it is often called, quantum mechanics…. Did I just hear some groans from you? Well, they would be justified. If you thought the two theories of relativity are hard to understand, just wait a few minutes until we get into describing the quantum.

When I started this section of the course, I was confused by what "quantum" really meant, so I looked it up in Wikipedia. It says that quantum is "a discrete quantity of energy proportional in magnitude to the frequency of the radiation it represents." Okay, that clears things up…You bet!... This definition really doesn't help me, so let's move on to what the course says.

The study of quantum mechanics is the study of nature at a very small scale, such as atoms and subatomic particles. I'm not going to get into any detail on all of the known subatomic particles and how they interact with each other, because it is quite complex and beyond the scope of what I'm trying to present. However, we will revisit some of them briefly at times as we move on from here.

Just like the theories of relativity looked at the universe at a very large "universal" scale, the study of quantum mechanics looks at the very small parts of nature in our universe. Prior to the turn of the 20th

century, there were many thoughts as to what "pieces" made up matter. By the start of the 20th century, it was fairly well agreed that matter was made up of atoms which were very small, and that they were made up of a positive electrically charged nucleus, and orbiting around the nucleus were smaller, negatively charged electrons. This was probably the model of the atom that you learned about when you were in high school. However, scientists found problems with this concept. According to Maxwell's equations, the electrons rotating around the nucleus should lose energy by radiating electromagnetic waves, just like a satellite rotating around the earth losing energy from friction, and then the electrons should spiral right into the nucleus. All this should happen in a split second, so atoms really should not exist at all, but they do. When I looked up atoms in Wikipedia, there was an explanation that even though electromagnetic energy is given off by the electron, some of the energy is converted into kinetic energy, which is the energy of motion, and this kinetic energy is what keeps the electrons in their orbit around the nucleus. Really? Well, there must be quite a bit of kinetic energy to keep all those electrons rotating in their orbits around the nucleus. In any event, it made me scratch my head.

Scientists also looked at light over the centuries, and asked, "Is light a particle or wave? Well, through many experiments, it was discovered that light can act like both. It was found that if you did experiments to show light as consisting of small particles, then you could show it. If you did experiments to show that light was a wave, you could show that as well. So, is quantum physics absurd? You would think so. It even left the early pioneers of this field with their doubts, but this "light" theory has been remarkably successful at explaining the world at the atomic and subatomic level. Scientists have also postulated that at the very small scales of observation, the actual process of making observations and measurements will actually affect the outcome. This is called quantization. For example, if you used photons or "particles" of light to "observe" an electron's velocity and position, the photon's contact with the electron will actually alter the electron's velocity or position, or perhaps both. This statement may not be completely scientifically correct, but it really does make the point that we humans may be limited in what we can ever know, or at least know at this time in scientific history, which certainly adds to the mystery of this great universe. To make matters more confusing, scientists have actually discovered that at the very small quantum level, atoms can actually be in two places at the same time! This quantum superposition is real, and recent experiments have shown this to be true. Once an observation is made, this "superposition" goes away, and you will observe the atom in one place or the other. If you are not making an observation, the atom can actually be in both places at the same time. Quantization is at play here, disturbing the results of those experiments. I guess we will have to believe what the scientists have to say on this matter. In any case, all of this information seems to defy "normal" logic, but I will take it at face value until better theories arise or evidence is provided to the contrary. Oh brother! My head is really itchy now. I better scratch it again.

At this point, I want to describe the double-slit or two-slit experiment that I find remarkable, which seems to show that light is a wave. Picture a piece of cardboard with two parallel slits cut into it vertically, fairly close together. Shine the light through both of the slits at the same time and you will see something strange on the wall opposite the two slits. You will see a series of light and dark vertical "stripes" of light spread out over the area on the wall opposite. What you are seeing is a wave interference pattern from the light going through the two slits. What is happening is that light is acting like a wave, going through each of the slits and radiating out through each slit like a water wave would radiate out when you drop a pebble in a dish of water. As each of these waves radiates out through each of their slits, the wave troughs and crests will meet each other and create smaller troughs and larger crests. This is what you see on the opposite wall. The brighter areas are where the light crests have met or joined, and the darker areas are where the light troughs joined together. I realize that this is hard to visualize, so I encourage you to look up wave interference patterns so you can see a visual example. I found that Wikipedia does a good job at illustrating this visually as well as giving you a much more technical explanation which is beyond the scope of what I'm trying to present here for you. Just search for "double-slit experiment" and "interference patterns of waves" to find Wikipedia explanations. That should get you started.

What about light acting like a particle? I spent a great deal of time looking for a decent explanation and finally found the following website, but even this explanation is not all that simple. It explains the photoelectric effect, which illustrates that light acts as a particle as well.

The following website from Las Cumbres Observatory explains the photoelectric effect:

https://lco.global/spacebook/light/light-particle/

But first, this is what Wikipedia says about the Las Cumbres Oservatory. "Las Cumbres Observatory is a network of astronomical observatories run by a non-profit private operating foundation directed by the technologist Wayne Rosing. Its offices are in Goleta, California. The telescopes are located at both northern and southern hemisphere sites distributed in longitude around the Earth. For some astronomical objects, the longitudinal spacing of telescopes allows continuous observations over 24 hours or longer."

The website states the following about the photoelectric effect:

'Light behaves mainly like a wave but it can also be considered to consist of tiny packages of energy called photons. Photons carry a fixed amount of energy but have no mass. The energy of a photon depends on its wavelength: longer wavelength photons have less energy and shorter wavelength photons have more. Red photons, for example, have less energy than blue ones.

Until about 1900, scientists only understood electromagnetic radiation to be made up of waves. Then Max Planck and others were studying the photoelectric effect and they found that certain types of metal and other materials will eject electrons when light shines on them. They expected that the number of electrons ejected from the metal would increase with the intensity or brightness of the light directed towards the metal. What they found instead, was that the wavelength of the light was what affected the number of electrons ejected.

More energetic wavelengths such as blue and ultraviolet caused more electrons to be ejected than red or infrared wavelengths. They also found that increasing the intensity of light increased the number of electrons ejected, but not their speed. Planck realized that the energy of the electromagnetic radiation was proportional to its frequency, but admitted that he didn't understand why this was the case and said it was lucky guesswork.

Einstein was the first to explain what was happening. He theorized that electromagnetic energy comes in packets, or quanta which we now call photons. So light behaves as a wave and as a particle, depending on the circumstances and the effect being observed. This concept is now known as wave-particle duality. Einstein won the 1921 Nobel Prize in Physics "for his services to

Theoretical Physics, and especially for his discovery of the law of the photoelectric effect".'

So, what can we get out of this explanation? First, photons are what I guess we can call the "particles" of light, and second, there are more of them striking the metal when the light has a higher frequency and knocking more electrons off of the metal plate than with light that has a lower frequency.

There you have it! Light can act like a particle. However, as we saw with the double-slit experiment, light also acts as a wave. Therefore, depending on the type of experiment you design, you can show that light is a particle or a wave, which as you can see, is an illustration of the wave-particle duality of light.

Before we leave the subject of light, there is one more thing to be said. The double or two-slit experiment has been done not just with light, but this phenomenon has been shown to occur for electrons, atoms and even some molecules – or in other words, matter. Think about that for a few seconds. What this means is that every object is not just matter made up of particles, but also a collection of waves. Your coffee cup, your car, your house, and even you all have wave properties! To me, that fact is amazing. How can that be? Well, the next section on the Higgs boson might help with an explanation of sorts. Just wait and see. However, this new information should change how you view the universe. I know it does for me. I never thought before that I was anything more than a few particles thrown together in a systematic way.

So, what does this say about the universe? Well, for one thing, it means that the universe is much more complex than we ever thought it could be, and certainly not as intuitively clear, either. This just shows you that all the brilliant scientists are finding their way through this complex universe just like you and I, one small piece of information at a time. It really makes you wonder just how many more pieces of information—or as the philosophers would say, truths—about this great universe there are to be discovered. There possibly could be an infinite amount of information yet to be discovered, which means that the universe is basically unknowable to mankind. Perhaps that is the way it should be. The human brain is marvelous and awesome, but as awesome as it is, perhaps it is reaching its limit at understanding this wonderous universe that we all live in. We'll be revisiting this point a time or two more before we end.

In any event, scientists are continuing their quests to find out more about our universe. They believe that there is a "theory of everything" which will require the merging of general relativity with quantum physics to make a theory of "quantum gravity." They just discovered the Higgs boson particle in 2012, which might help in their quests, and which we will talk about next.

Chapter 12

THE HIGGS BOSON

*T*took the Great Course The Higgs Boson and Beyond, which was taught by Professor Sean Carroll of the California Institute of Technology. There has been so much talk about the Higgs boson since 2012 that I thought I should learn a bit more about it. In the news they were hailing it as the "God Particle," but that really isn't the case, unless you consider all particles in the universe as God particles. The course was published in 2015, which was a while after the last course I took about relativity and quantum mechanics, which has a copyright date of 2000. You would think that science has advanced in the last ten or fifteen years, and you would be right.

Right away at the beginning of the second lecture, Professor Carroll states that "the world, at a fundamental level, is made up fields, and the rules of quantum mechanics say that when we look at those fields, we see them as particles." He continues by stating that particles are really just excitations or vibrations in quantum fields, or let's just say fields. When we observe a particle or particles, what we are really see-ing is a field or fields that are vibrating. There is no particle that exists, but it looks like there is one. In the last course, there was no definitive

149

statement that particles were really excitations of fields. That course just simply showed us the wave-particle duality, and that depending on what we were looking for, we would see either a wave or particle, based on the experiment's design. Professor Carroll seems to have cleared up the question of this wave-particle duality by stating that everything we see is not a specific piece of matter but just some "excited fields" vibrating, allowing us to see this as "matter."

Professor Carroll definitively states that light is a wave and not a particle. In the case of light it is the electromagnetic field that is doing the "waving." Within the waves there may be vibrations of the fields at points which we will observe as particles. You could say that our eyes are tricking us into believing that there really is something there when in fact there isn't. There is just an excited field.

The idea of fields has been around for a very long time, but it was scientists that studied these fields over the years that pointed us in the direction of "quantum field theory." If there was a vibration of a field, then you would see something. If there was no vibration of a field, then you would not see anything. What our eyes do is to resolve these vibrations into something called particles. We still use the term "particles" even though they don't exist, because it is an easy way to identify the various vibrations of fields in the universe, and there are many fields in this universe. Some of the particles that scientists have discovered over the years are: W Bosons, Z Bosons, Up-type quarks, Down-type quarks, gluons, photons, tau leptons, muon leptons, tau neutrinos, muon neutrinos, electrons, etc. The Higgs boson is the most recent particle discovered, but please realize that there may be many other particles yet to be discovered if the universe allows us to find them. Who knows? There may be an infinite number.

In any event, what is this Higgs field? Well, the Higgs field is yet another field, but this field is unique in that it gives mass to other particles.

For example, imagine a would-be massless electron moving through space. If the Higgs field were not present, then the electron would be moving at the speed of light. However, since the Higgs field is present the electron "feels" its presence, and that is what gives it mass. I like to think that the electron is running through a field of goop or as the kids would say, slime, and as a result, this slime slows the electron down so it can't reach the speed of light. I'm sure that particle physicists would have a problem with that description, but it sure helps me to understand the concept. So, what is this mass? The course says that mass is the intrinsic property of a particle or object, and that inertial mass is the resistance to acceleration, and that the Higgs field gives this inertial mass to particles. There is also gravitational mass, but that is not related to the Higgs field. I like to think of gravitational mass as the amount a particle or object "bends" the spacetime continuum.

Scientists speculated about the existence of this Higgs field for a long time, so how did they discover it? Well, they built the Large Hadron Collider (LHC) on the French-Swiss border, with about seventy countries participating in various ways, financially and scientifically. It is a huge machine that is 27 kilometers in circumference. What they did was to smash protons together by running them into each other in this huge machine. They discovered the Higgs boson particle not by detecting it directly, because the Higgs boson decays very rapidly, but by the byproducts of this decay of the Higgs particle. Quite a bit of the course is taken up with how the various particles and fields interact with each other and create vibrations or particles in other fields, and it explains how the scientists were able to discover this new particle—or we should say, the excitation of the Higgs field through the excitations of the various other particle fields. They knew that smashing protons together would create this new particle because of their years of research and experiments with all the other particles that they discovered. There is quite a bit of material in this course about these other particles, and all the other particle accelerators and detectors in the world, so I recommend that you take this course if you are interested in getting more detail about the world of particle physics. Quite frankly, a lot of the course went over my head, because I fear that the professor tried to explain a whole scientific field in a short twelve-half-hour lecture course. Perhaps you will have better luck.

The last two lecture courses pretty much explained in detail that there is a lot about the universe that we don't know. Scientists will more than likely learn a lot more about it, but even when they do – is there an infinite amount of information to be learned about this great universe? If so, we will never learn everything that there is to know, and maybe that's the way it should be.

Chapter 13

THE THEORY OF
EVERYTHING

*W*ell, we are at the last scientific course that I will explain for our benefit. Yes, there are many other scientific courses that I could take to help explain the universe around us, but I actually think that with the three science-related courses I'm presenting here, we can get a good enough sense of how the knowledge of the universe as it is today can or cannot play a role in furthering our understanding of human spirituality, or our sense of God from a scientific point of view. Already, we have seen just how awesome our world is, from what the various scientists over the centuries have discovered, but it is clear that there is much more that we could learn about the universe. Even if there isn't an infinite amount more of information to be learned about the universe, will mankind ever know everything that there is to know about it? I really doubt it, because after taking this course, I really don't think man will ever know everything that there is to know.

The course is The Great Course called The Theory of Everything: The Quest to Explain All Reality. It is taught by Professor Don Lincoln of the Fermi National Accelerator Laboratory. He is also a guest speaker on High Energy Physics at the University of Notre Dame, and he received his Ph.D. in Experimental Particle Physics from Rice University. He was also a member of the team that discovered the top quark in 1995 and a member of the team that confirmed the existence of the Higgs boson in 2012. He has published many books and articles as well as given hundreds of lectures on four continents. The copyright date of this course is 2017, so it is the most current of the three scientific courses that I'm covering for you here. However, if you are reading this in ten, fifteen, twenty, or more years from that date, then perhaps some of the information presented from these three scientific courses may have changed, and you should take everything I'm saying with a grain of salt and perhaps get updated on the scientific events of the times.

The first thing that I want to say after taking this course on The Theory of Everything is that there is so much more to be learned about the universe despite our advances in the twentieth century with particle physics and the two theories of relativity. It appears that there are thousands of scientists working day and night, in many different areas of scientific thought, just to add little bits and pieces to our understanding of the universe, and just from my ordinary man point of view I really don't see that even if there are a great number of major discoveries in the next few decades, that these revelations will do anything but just put a dent in our knowledge of this great universe we live in on this small planet we call earth. I would say that is the biggest "take away" I got out of this course by Don Lincoln. The amount of knowledge that is still left to be learned about the universe has left me in awe.

There was a lot of material presented in this course, but quite a bit of it was covered to some degree by Professor Wolfson and Professor Carroll in the previous two science courses explained already. Therefore, I will try my best not to repeat too many of the facts.

Before I get into covering some of the material presented by Professor Lincoln, there is one difference that I want to address. Both Professor Wolfson and Professor Lincoln in their discussions talk about particles and waves as if they are two separate entities. However, as you recall, Professor Carroll definitively states that "the world, at a fundamental level, is made up fields, and the rules of quantum mechanics say that when we look at those fields, we see them as particles." He continues by stating that particles are really just excitations or vibrations in quantum fields. So, as I see it, waves are created by the movement of these quantum fields and radiate out in all directions, but at specific points where there is intense vibration, what we see as a particle is in fact a very excited field vibrating at that point. I'm not sure if a particle physicist would completely agree with that statement, but in my simple and ordinary mind, it is the best way to wrap my head around this difficult concept. In any event, I'm sure Professors Wolfson and Lincoln see it the same way as Professor Carroll, but since this concept is so difficult to explain in a course, they may have decided to let the particle-wave duality stand on its own and not to go off on a tangent that might be off the point of their course presentations.

Professor Lincoln starts off the course by stating that in order to start developing a theory of everything there needs to be, at a minimum, a unification of Einstein's general theory of relativity (theory of gravity) and the standard model of particle physics (quantum mechanics/quantum physics). As of now, there is no unification that has been discovered.

He presents the five known forces in the universe:

Gravity, where objects are drawn to each other—or as we saw already, gravity is the curvature of spacetime.

Electromagnetism, which covers electricity, magnetism, light, and chemistry.

The strong force, which binds the protons and neutrons together in the nucleus of atoms.

The weak force, which is responsible for some forms of radioactivity, such as the decay of atoms.

The Higgs field, which gives mass to subatomic particles.

Scientists have been trying to find out how these forces can be unified in some way, in the quest for a theory of everything. In the late 1960s, they found out that electromagnetism and the weak force were two facets of the same thing, which they called the electroweak force, and since the Higgs field is tied up with the electroweak force, perhaps it can be included in the electroweak umbrella. However, it appears that there has not been much further progress in this area.

These forces play a big role in how all the "particles" of the universe interact with each other. I will continue to use the term "particle" because Professor Lincoln uses it throughout the course; however, I have adopted Professor Carroll's definition of a particle being a vibration of a subatomic field.

Later in the course, Professor Lincoln talks about the force of gravity a bit more. Of these known forces, gravity is the weakest. The electromagnetic, strong, and weak forces are much stronger than gravitational forces, relatively speaking. We know that as the distances between two objects increase greatly, the gravitational force between those objects drops off very sharply. Why is this the case? Some scientists have speculated that gravity may be as strong as the other forces except that gravity is not just operating in our three dimensions. It may be operating in four, five, or more other dimensions which makes it look weak in our three-dimensional world. These dimensions would probably be very small. For example, think of these dimensions as in the following analogy. Let's say that an observer on another planet in another galaxy many light years from earth observes our earth. To that observer, earth would look like a one-dimensional point, but earth is actually round and people move up, down, and sideways on the surface. However, our observer in another galaxy cannot see that at all. To that observer, all he sees is a tiny point. Likewise, on our earth, another observer at the same time could be looking at a small round rock at a very great distance. To that observer, the rock would look like a small one-dimensional point off in the great distance. However, it is round, and a small bug could go up, down, and around that rock, which our earth observer cannot see. In any case, hopefully this analogy gives you some sense of what these small extra dimensions could actually be like, and we could go on and on with various observers at each of the progressively smaller scales. Please note that this description is just an analogy to help you understand the concept of extra dimensions. I am not actually saying that this example *is* the extra dimensions. So, what about gravity? Could it be operating in multiple dimensions, thus making its force look weak to us? There is no way to know for sure, because there is zero evidence that extra dimensions exist. It is just a thought that some scientists have raised.

A great majority of this course is spent describing the subatomic particles of the standard model of particle physics and how they interact with each other and the forces that act on them. In this course, Professor Lincoln goes into more detail about all these known particles than Professor Carroll did in his course. There was quite a bit of information in both courses about the standard model of particle physics, which described their interactions or non-interactions with each other, their stability or decay, radioactivity generated, energy released from their interactions with each other, etc. There was discussion about symmetries in the universe in this course, where symmetry is defined as the ability to change something and you would see no changes. This discussion centered around the standard model of particle physics and the changes that could occur or not occur. However, I am not going to go into any detail describing this great wealth of information on particle physics for two reasons. First of all, quite a bit of it was beyond my ability to comprehend this detail without a great deal of further study in particle physics, and if I tried to describe more detail of what was presented I was afraid that I would not represent the information correctly. Second, and more important, if I went into greater detail, I think it would take away from what I am trying to present to us ordinary people. Suffice it to say that the universe with all its particles is a wondrous thing and very complicated. It leaves me wondering where all these particles came from and why. I suspect we will never know.

Before we move on from these particles, we need to mention that there are other "particle" types that were or are possibly present in the universe. For each "particle" type in the standard model, such as electrons, quarks, bosons, etc. there is also an opposite "sister particle" type, which are called antimatter particles. Scientists don't know much about antimatter, but we know it is the opposite of matter. If the two are combined, a great amount of energy is released. The opposite is also true. Energy can be turned into matter and antimatter particles. What is important to understand is that you need equal amounts of each type of matter for this great energy release to occur. There is a problem when we look at the formation of the universe 14 billion years ago. Scientists know that the early universe was filled with a lot of energy and it was much smaller and hotter than it is today. According to the Big Bang theory, when the universe "exploded" into existence spontaneously, this energy created matter and antimatter particles equally. When the two types combined, they would have annihilated each other and there should only be energy left in the universe. However, this is not the case. So, why does only ordinary matter exist naturally in large quantities. Scientists think that there may be some other kind of physics in the universe that we don't understand that somehow allowed the formation of ordinary matter. It's just another question for scientific research. However, we do know that antimatter creation occurs naturally in high-energy processes involving cosmic rays, and also in high-energy experiments in accelerators on earth. So, there is antimatter in the universe that is created naturally and experimentally. It's just not created in large quantities. A lot is left to be learned about these particles.

To make things even more confusing, there is yet another kind of matter called dark matter. So what is the difference between antimatter and dark matter? Well, I looked it up on the internet at a Bing site, and this is what is described.

"Dark matter and antimatter are two forms of matter, which are least, understood. Dark matter is a form of matter, which is not observable through the electromagnetic spectrum but only observable through the gravitational interactions. Antimatter is a form of matter, which is the 'negative,' or the 'opposite' of matter."

What I take away from this explanation is that antimatter is a lot like our ordinary matter in that it can be shown to exist, even if it isn't in great quantities, through experimentation. However, dark matter cannot be "seen," at least at this time, through our scientific endeavors. Scientists have a theory of its existence because there has to be something to hold the universe's galaxies together. If we look at only the ordinary matter in the universe, there isn't enough matter to provide the gravitational force to necessarily hold these galaxies together. If only ordinary matter is present providing the gravitational force, then these galaxies should tear themselves apart, and the ordinary matter would be thrown out into space. This does not happen; therefore, there has to be some "other" matter present that provides the gravitational forces to keep these galaxies intact. This is the unproven theory that scientists have at present and they call this matter "dark matter."

There you have it! Ordinary matter made up of the particles of the standard model of particle physics, antimatter which are the sisters of the particles of ordinary matter, and lastly dark matter, which no one knows much about at this time except for its gravitational force. These seem to be the only pieces of matter that we know about now. Are you confused? I know that I am, and all this talk of matter leaves me wondering: Are there other types of yet undiscovered matter in existence? This is similar to the question of whether there are other particle "types" yet to be discovered.

However, before we leave this topic of matter, there is a theory called superstring theory which theorizes that all of our standard ordinary particles in existence are actually one-dimensional "objects" shaped like strings of spaghetti or little hula hoops in perhaps ten dimensions. Yes! Multiple dimensions, again. It appears that this theory holds out mathematically when there are ten dimensions (three spatial, one of time, and six other dimensions) in order to make the theory believable. In any case, the theory speculates that these strings vibrate in certain ways to become what we know as our standard particles. For example, perhaps one string might vibrate one way to appear as a quark. Another string might vibrate another way to appear as an electron, and so on for all of our standard particles. This theory seems to be more closely aligned with what Professor Carroll states, that particles are really just vibrating fields. Perhaps they are just vibrating string "objects," which still could only be vibrating fields that look like "objects." As a clarification, the above are my thoughts not the scientist's thoughts. In any case, scientists have a lot more work to do on this theory if it is to be generally accepted.

At this point, I think I will leave this talk of matter and particles, at least for now, as it relates to what was presented in this course. I'll leave it to you to do further investigation if you so desire. However, in a little bit, I want to explain a phenomenon called quantum entanglement, which involves our subatomic particle friends, after I've finished with this course description. So, we are not quite finished with these pesky particles yet.

Moving on, Professor Lincoln talks about the expansion of the universe. Just about everyone has heard of the Big Bang theory, where the universe was a very tiny dot that "exploded" into existence about 14 billion years ago. The universe expanded, and there were several ideas about this expansion. First, there was the idea that the universe would expand constantly forever. It might slow down, but it would never stop its expansion. Secondly, there was the idea that the universe would expand for a while and then just stop its expansion and stay still at some point. Lastly, some scientists thought that after a time of expansion the universe would turn around and start collapsing in on itself due to all the gravity. Clearly, this is a very disturbing scenario for any life in existence in the universe at the time. However, in 1998, two groups of scientists discovered that the rate of expansion of the universe was actually accelerating. How could this be the case? A new theory was devised. There was something called dark energy in the universe (which should not be confused with dark matter) that was causing this accelerating expansion. Scientists are pretty sure that this energy exists, and even more surprising, that it is of a constant density throughout the universe, which means that as the expansion continues, the amount of dark energy is also increasing at an accelerated rate. At this time, it is estimated that the universe is composed of about 70% dark energy, 5% ordinary matter, and 25% dark matter. As you can see, our simple ordinary particles are way outnumbered by all this "dark stuff" in the universe that we know very little about at this time. Perhaps over time we will learn more.

The last thing I want to talk about from this course is the concept of multiverses or multiple universes. This is only a hypothesis of scientists. There is no proof that they exist, but the idea is very intriguing. Basically, this is the concept that there are parallel universes in existence right beside our universe, but we cannot see them. Perhaps they are infinite in number, or perhaps not. In any case, we can think that maybe these other universes operate by different laws of physics. For example, in our universe, $E=mc^2$, but in another universe this equation might be different, or maybe there is no such thing as light in it. Professor Lincoln in this course also corrected a misconception about the equation $E=mc^2$ in our universe. He stated that this equation holds if the object has no momentum. In other words, it is stationary. If the object has momentum, then the equation is a bit more complex, but we are not going to get into that here. Please take the course if you want to learn more about it and some other interesting facts and details about our universe. Continuing on, we see that in our universe the Higgs field gives mass to our particles, but in another universe, there might be no such thing as a Higgs field. I think you can get a good idea of what I am saying, and that life as we know it here may not be able to survive in another universe, because the rules and laws of physics may be different. There is even a theory that within our universe a "bubble" could develop and start inflating spontaneously and create a universe in that way or that at various places in our own universe the laws of physics are different, thus creating a kind of "new" universe of sorts. You could say that the mathematics of science there could be different.

I'm not sure how multiple dimensions relate to multiverses. Perhaps they are some sort of "barrier" between universes, or perhaps they exist separately within each universe. I don't know, but it certainly gives us all something to think about.

In the very last lecture, Professor Lincoln basically summarizes what he has presented in the course and concludes that a lot more work has to be done before we get close to some sort of theory of everything. As I mentioned at the beginning of this section, there is so much to be learned about the world we live in that I really don't think mankind will ever be able to solve the riddles of the universe or multiple universes, if they exist. There is just too much to be discovered, and if there is an infinite amount of information to be learned... well... it would be impossible to learn it all. We may need to be content to accept whatever bits and pieces we do learn, be in awe of the enormity of the world we live in, and recognize that we might never learn everything there is to know.

Lastly, I realize in these last few pages I presented a whole lot of information in a very short space. I recommend that you reread it a time or two. If you do, then I think you will see that our universe is absolutely amazing and will leave you scratching your head, as it did for me. It made me feel very small indeed.

Chapter 14

BEFORE WE CLOSE OUT OUR STUDY OF SCIENCE

There are just a couple more things that I want to mention before we end the science presentations.

First, let's get back to those pesky subatomic particles. There is a phenomenon called quantum entanglement. I found a short article that seems to explain it in a fairly simple manner, but even at that, it is a hard concept to explain and understand. This is what I found at:

https://www.cnet.com/news/physicists-prove-einsteins-spooky-quantum-entanglement/

'Few things in science get crazier than quantum mechanics, with related theories sometimes sounding more like paranormal activity than physics. So when such theories gain experimental proof it's a big day for physicists.

Quantum entanglement is a curious phenomenon that occurs when two particles remain connected, even over large distances, in such a way that actions performed on one particle have an effect on the other. For instance, one particle might be spun in a clockwise direction. The result on the second particle would be an equal anti-clockwise spin.

Three different research papers claim to have closed loopholes in 50-year-old experiments that demonstrate quantum entanglement, proving its existence more definitively than ever before.

"Things get really interesting when two electrons become entangled," said Ronald Hanson from the University of Delft. "They are perfectly correlated, when you observe one, the other one will always be opposite. That effect is instantaneous, even if the other electron is in a rocket at the other end of the galaxy."'

Scientists have tested this phenomenon many times, and it seems that if one connected subatomic particle is doing "something" at one end of the galaxy, the other connected particle mimics its action at the other end of the galaxy in the opposite direction. Distance does not seem to matter here. If you think about it, we said that nothing can go faster than the speed of light, yet somehow the actions of a particle a great distance away seem to influence another particle at the same time, though even the speed of light could not reach the other particle to provide this instantaneous reaction. What's going on here? Is there some other kind of physics in the universe that we don't know about that can explain these occurrences? Well, let's just say that this is yet another mystery that the universe has locked up for us at this time in the history of our world.

Secondly, what about chaos theory? For the last few weeks, I oscillated back and forth on whether or not I should bring it up. I wasn't sure if it would provide anything interesting to say on our subject of God, religion, or spirituality. After some thought, I think it might say something.

I thought about taking The Great Course on this subject, but then I looked at a few different web sites on the subject. This one seemed to present the most simplified and easy to understand explanation, so I went with it: https://simple.wikipedia.org/wiki/Chaos_theory

Here's what it said:

'Chaos theory is a part of mathematics. It looks at certain systems that are very sensitive. A very small change may make the system behave completely differently.

Very small changes in the starting position of a chaotic system make a big difference after a while. This is why even large computers cannot tell the weather for more than a few days in the future. Even if the weather was perfectly measured, a small change or error will make the prediction completely wrong. Since even a butterfly can make enough wind to change weather, a chaotic system is sometimes called the "butterfly effect". No computer knows enough to tell how the small wind will change the weather.

Some systems (like weather) might appear random at first look, but chaos theory says that these kinds of systems or patterns may not be. If people pay close enough attention to what is really going on, they might notice the chaotic patterns.

The main idea of chaos theory is that a minor difference at the start of a process can make a major change in it as time progresses.'

What this tells me is that, in a very complex system like weather pre-diction, absolutely no one can predict exactly what the weather will be like at a specific time or place. However, there may be patterns to the weather that can be observed. For example, no one can say that at exactly 1:35 p.m. on 5/5/2019 it will start raining. However, observa-tion may show that with a cold front and warm front merging over the area sometime during the day on 5/5/2019, there will probably be rain at some point in the day. This pattern of cold and warm fronts merg-ing, as observed many times in the past, can predict that there is a high probability of rain coming. Therefore, I see chaos theory as a kind of mathematical study of probabilities, based on previous observations of a system such as the weather. We don't know what is going to happen at a particular time and place, but based on previously observed patterns, we might get a pretty good idea of what is going to happen.

There is also a study of chaos theory at the quantum level. Needless to say, we are not going there, because I have a hard enough time under-standing some of the aspects of the standard model of particle physics that if I had to add the patterns of chaos theory to it, my mind might actually explode.

So what does this chaos theory have to do with spirituality? Let's look at how an early farmer in much earlier times might look at nature. He has no knowledge of science or the study of weather patterns. He just knows that if he plants in the spring, then later in the year he can harvest his crop, as long as there is enough rain and sunshine. Let's also suppose that there is a drought in that particular year. His crop is dying. Where is the rain? So, this early farmer may pray to his God for rain. Eventually, the rain comes, and his crop survives. He attributes his success to divine intervention; however, in actuality the weather pattern was changing from that of drought to a more seasonal pattern. He doesn't know that, so he gives praise and sacrifices to his God or gods.

What does this example say? It says that knowledge is power. If this farmer had at his disposal all of the advances of science, then he might not be so inclined to say that his success was due to divine intervention. Would he be an atheist? Probably not, because there are just so many other things about the world that he doesn't know about during his time. That sounds just like the rest of us. Science has found a whole lot of information about our world and universe, but as we have seen, there is a huge amount of information yet to be discovered. How do we resolve this lack of knowledge? Well, quite a few people, including brilliant scientists past and present, turn to religion, God, or spirituality to calm their concerns about what they don't know. For example, here are a few great scientists that have deep spiritual roots. It doesn't mean they are ignoring their scientific observations. I believe it just means that they know that they don't have all the answers, and they turn to their spirituality for comfort.

Father Georges Le Maitre (1894-1966) – He was a mathematician, astronomer and professor of physics. He was the first to identify the expanding universe, and the first to propose the Big Bang theory of the creation of the universe.

William Thompson, 1st Baron Kelvin (1824-1907) – He was a brilliant mathematician and scientist who discovered the 1st and 2nd laws of thermodynamics. Thompson was a devout believer in Christianity

(Scottish Episcopal) and attendance at chapel was part of his daily routine.

Johannes Kepler (1571-1630) – He was a mathematician and astronomer best known for his laws of planetary motion. He believed that God created the world according to an intelligible plan that is accessible through the natural light of reason.

This information was found at catholicscientists.org, but there are many more examples of scientists who are religious or spiritual. I will not present them here because you can easily find information on them at that website, as well as other sites on the web.

Well, here we are, we are at the end of our research on science. On reflection, there are a great many things science has told us that are hard to understand. Nothing can go faster than the speed of light. Time slows down the faster you are going. Gravity is actually the 'bending' of the spacetime continuum. Black Holes are really scary strong forces of gravity. The interaction of the subatomic particles of the standard model of particle physics is very complex. Additionally, science has also proposed a lot of theories, thoughts, and questions about the universe as well. Do multiple dimensions exist? Do multiple universes exist? Why does quantum entanglement exist? Will the universe stop expanding and collapse in on itself? Why do dark matter and dark energy exist, if in fact they really do exist?

We could go on listing the things that we know and do not know, but suffice it to say that there just is so much more to learn about our world, and it may be endless. In the meantime, we just need to accept our place in this world and be in awe of its magnificence.

Our Reality

REDEFINING REALITY:
THE INTELLECTUAL
IMPLICATIONS OF
MODERN SCIENCE

$\mathcal{W}$e are now getting close to the finish line of our course studies. The last course from The Great Courses that I will be presenting to you is the course that is named by the title above. It is a philosophy course that discusses some of the questions of our universe from a scientific point of view. I felt it was a good way to move forward from our scientific studies and move into an area where we can look at the implications of what science has shown us.

The course has a copyright date of 2015, so the scientific information is fairly current. It is taught by Professor Steven Gimbel of Gettysburg College, where he serves as the chair of the philosophy department. He has received various teaching awards, and he has published numerous articles and four books. I found this course very fascinating and went through it in record time, because I couldn't wait to find out the next discovery that he was about to present.

In the process of writing about this course, I attempted not to repeat what I have already presented. Professor Gimbel provides great detail in his course about the many scientific areas that we have already studied, so instead I hope to add a philosophical perspective to that information. You be the judge of whether I have succeeded.

The course looked at how science has shaped and reshaped our sense of reality and the ways in which these changes have "influenced the way we live, our interaction with each other and the artifacts we create. Scientists give us new accounts of how the universe works, and philosophers unpack those theories to see what they tell us about what is real." For example, in early science the human body was considered a machine that ran according to the laws of early physics. If someone became sick it was just thought that there was something wrong with the workings of the machine. This was the common belief prior to the 20th and 21st centuries. This was their reality. However, newer science provided a new hypothesis. Through the work of Frenchman Louis Pasteur, the germ theory of illness became accepted as the new reality. It was discovered that maybe the machine itself wasn't malfunctioning; perhaps it was germs and bacteria that were causing some of the illnesses in people. Scientists focused on these germs and bacteria and found ways to make vaccines to eradicate many illnesses, such as smallpox and polio. A new reality as it related to illness was emerging, and today many other germ-related illnesses have been successfully treated. However, some of these nasty germs are evolving and discovering ways to counter our medicines, so the battle continues. One example is the COVID-19 pandemic in 2020 that has shut down much of global commerce and has caused a great deal of fear in the global population. A vaccine has not been developed as of the fall of 2020, but we are all hopeful that one will be found soon.

The above example illustrates what Thomas Kuhn's book *The Structure of Scientific Revolutions* says about how humans tackle problems in science. I have not read the book, but Professor Gimbel pointed out from the book that science develops according to a set of rules for that time to tackle a particular scientific endeavor with the accepted tools of that time. For the most part, the tools help solve problems, but there will probably be anomalies that pop up. As time goes on, there may be more and more anomalies that appear, and then the scientists can no longer ignore these inconsistencies. Then the unthinkable happens! The scientists have to be revolutionary. They have to consider and then research new answers. This was the process that led to the germ theory of illness. Over time, scientists have discovered that there are not only bad germs but good ones as well. Let's just hope that the good ones always outnumber the bad ones, for our health's sake. There are over 100 trillion good bacteria in your gut right now, working to break down certain chemicals that we eat into a form that our body can absorb and make us healthy. We have come a long way from the view that the body is just a machine to the view that our body is a complex bio-organism that has many parts and pieces that all have separate functions that, when working properly, make us healthy.

Professor Gimbel talked about mathematics and the fact that everyone seems to think about mathematical laws and rules as absolute, and that these rules and laws are true everywhere. However, is this really a fact? He gave some good examples, but I think I will use another very simple example from my training as a mathematics major at Norwich University in the early 1970s to show that things may not be as they seem.

Draw a triangle. Measure each of the three angles of the triangle and add them together. You should get the sum as 180 degrees. This is always true, no matter how you draw the triangle. However, take a small ball and draw a triangle on it. Now measure the angles. When you add them up you will notice that their sum is greater than 180 degrees. The first example is from Euclidean geometry, where our environment as we know it is basically flat. Even though the earth is curved, we don't notice it, because the earth is so large and appears flat to us. Since everything around us seems flat, when we draw a triangle on these flat surfaces ,the sum of their angles will always add up to 180 degrees. The second example is from non-Euclidean geometry, where our environment is not strictly flat. It is curved; therefore we get a different result, and the sum of the angles is greater than 180 degrees. This illustrates to us that even the laws of mathematics can be different. These laws are established based on our environment. Change the environment, or our understanding of the environment, and the rules change. This should sound familiar. Think of Newtonian physics versus the physics of Einstein. For the most part, Newton's laws work, but occasionally they got things wrong. When Einstein developed his General Theory of Relativity, it showed that gravity wasn't a force between two objects, but rather it was the curvature of space and time by mass and energy. This difference in the laws of physics sounds similar to the differences between Euclidean and non-Euclidean geometry. If you think about it, since in physics the move from Newtonian physics to that of Einstein was a matter of learning more about our environment and finding that the rules of Einstein better fit our understanding of the universe. Could this be the same for geometry? Even though the rules of Euclidean geometry better fit our everyday lives here on earth, should we start to think that non-Euclidean geometry may actually be a better mathematical fit for our view of our place in the universe and reality? What does a better mathematical fit really mean, and is it really that important to the understanding of our universe? You decide.

In the next several lectures, Professor Gimbel explains some of the material we have already covered, such as the special and general theories of relativity, atoms, subatomic particles, quantum mechanics, quantum field theory, chaos theory, dark matter, dark energy, and the search for a theory of everything. I will not revisit these areas in detail, because they have been covered, but I do want to mention a couple of things that became a little clearer.

First, it became clearer to me that gravity is not just the curvature of the spacetime continuum by a mass, but by energy as well. Please recall that we previously learned that particles or massive objects really don't exist, instead all of our reality of particles is just our observation of fields vibrating. This vibration releases energy which appears to cause a curvature of the spacetime continuum and then we see this vibration as a particle. So, remember mass and energy are basically the same thing. He also stated that one can think of gravity as acceleration because when objects are close there is an acceleration towards each other, and the curvature of the spacetime continuum causes this acceleration of objects or particles towards each other.

Professor Gimbel also talked about the wave-particle duality of light. He pointed out what Einstein had said, that "light behaves like a particle only when it is emitted or absorbed. When it travels, it exhibits wave behavior. Is it a particle or a wave?" Let's stop and think about this for a minute and put a few things together that we have learned so far. Please recall that Professor Sean Carroll introduced us to quantum field theory, where particles are really just vibrations in fields, and there are many fields in the universe. Also recall that light travels through the electromagnetic field as waves. In the double-slit experiment, we saw that light traveled through the two slits, and then we saw the results of the waves traveling through these slits, where the waves from each slit caused the interference patterns that we could observe. In the photoelectric effect experiment, we could observe the electrons being bounced off of the metal when the photons knocked them off. So, can we think the following? As light travels through the electromagnetic field, it acts as a wave, as Einstein said, but when light hits the metal, it is acting like a particle called a photon and is absorbed by the metal. At the point of contact, the light wave hits the metal and no longer is a wave as we would normally think of a wave, such as a water wave hitting the shore. This contact causes a severe vibration in the electromagnetic field, which we could say is a photon particle making contact with the metal, and this vibration also causes a vibration of an electron in the metal that knocks this electron particle in another direction. Since we saw that all matter also has wave properties from other double-slit experiments that were conducted by scientists, then we could say that the electron is bounced off as a vibration of its field and travels as a wave as well. Is this an example of fields making contact with each other? Can we think of quantum field theory as a set of fields, and that these fields may or may not interact with each other? Can we also say that when waves of these fields travel, we don't observe anything except perhaps for interference patterns, but when these waves "hit" something, we see particles because the field is now vibrating? This description may not be entirely correct from a scientific point of view, but it helps me to put the whole concept of quantum field theory in perspective. Everything is a field, and when there are vibrations in fields, we "see" particles.

There is one last thought I have on quantum field theory. Superposition! Recall that this is when a particle can be in two places at the same time, but when you make an observation, the particle appears only at the place of observation. Could it be that when a field is vibrating in two places at the same time, the particle is thought to be at two different positions at the same time? However, then we make an observation and we only see that one particle. Could it be that in the process of observation we don't see the other area vibrating, even though it still is vibrating? Could it be that our observation blinds us to the other part of the field still vibrating? Are we being tricked into thinking that the particle is in two places at the same time before our observation, when in fact there are actually two particles vibrating? It's a thought. I'm sure a scientist out there can either refute or confirm this thought, so please do.

There is so much more to quantum field theory, and I invite you to research it more if it suits you. However, I feel that what I have presented will be enough to give a flavor of the essence of this theory without causing too much confusion for us non-scientists and ordinary people. Quite frankly, I think I have had enough of those pesky quantum particles for now and will leave it to the scientists to make further discoveries.

Let's move on to what Professor Gimbel has to say about chaos theory. Please recall that in a nutshell chaos theory says that in, a very complex system, a very small change in one variable can cause a large change in the outcome of what will happen in the system. Chaotic systems may seem random at first, but if you look closely enough, you may notice the patterns. Professor Gimbel clarified how we should think of chaotic systems with the following: "Chaotic systems are still deterministic systems. The present determines the future with absolute certainty. Nothing could be otherwise. The lack of predictability comes from our inability to measure as precisely as we need to and from the difficulty of the mathematics." There you have it! The present conditions will always determine the outcome. We just can't measure precisely enough because of our human limitations to see what the outcome will be. This kind of sounds like our experience with quantum mechanics. Where have we heard something like this before? Oh, yes. I wrote about making certain measurements of an electron: "Scientists have also postulated that at the very small scales of observation the actual process of making observations and measurements will actually affect the outcome. This is called quantization. For example, if you used photons or 'particles' of light to 'observe' an electron's velocity and position the photon's contact with the electron will actually alter the electron's velocity or position or perhaps both." In other words, we are limited in our abilities to make many different types of measurements, whether it is with a chaotic system or the position and velocity of an electron at any time in space. Let's face it! Humans are quite limited in their abilities to make measurements of complex systems or of things in the universe that are very small. Will we ever be able to make some of these measurements? At this point in human history, I suspect not, but you never know what new developments and tools will arise in science in the future.

From this point on in the course, Professor Gimbel presents material that is new to us. He next talks about our brain as a very complex system of neurons that we cannot really understand that well. As you will recall from our course on philosophy that Professor Patrick Grimm taught, I stated the following: "The neurons in our brains receive analog inputs and then provide outputs as digital. As an example, a dimmer on a light switch can change the intensity of the light's brightness. This is an example of an analog input. You can then imagine that this dimmer can be an input to a program that measures the intensity, and if it reaches a certain level will produce a charge that is then used elsewhere digitally." You can see that the brain is not a simple human organ. A lot of things are going on in our brains at any given time. Professor Gimbel in this course then speculates that perhaps our consciousness, which is determined by the actions of brain functions, is something like quantum superposition. The brain is so complex that our consciousness is in a superposed state until it is acted upon by the chemical environment of the brain, which causes the superposed state to collapse and fire off a particular constellation of neurons to give us a set of memories, thoughts, or actions to perform. Since this is occurring at the quantum level, it is hard to tell what the outcome will be and what the superposed state will collapse into. So, does this quantum "randomness" give us a sense of free will? Do we determine for ourselves what our actions will be? I tend to think not, at this time. When the superposed states exist and then collapse, there are very many outcomes that could occur. I don't see that we are in control of the outcome in any way. It seems rather random to me. Professor Gimbel may not agree with me, but I believe we are functioning at the whim of the universe. Whatever it has in store for us will be. So the question remains, is there intelligence to what the universe is doing? I doubt if we will ever know.

Professor Gimbel moves on to biological factors that affect our reality. Evolution and genes play a large part in who we are and what we will become. Human beings evolved over thousands of years to become the creature at the top of the food chain, but Darwin says that we really are just animals, in the end. We need to survive, and in order to do that, we need to keep any empathetic or sympathetic tendencies for others in check lest we become food for others. When genes and DNA were discovered recently, we found that we all inherited the traits of our families, both the good and bad. In the mid-20th century there were people who wanted to see if we could genetically remove these "bad" traits. This was called eugenics. In the beginning, eugenics wasn't an evil plan to alter human beings. At first, there were well- intentioned people that wanted to help remove suffering from the world. However, the situation must have changed. This is what Wikipedia has to say about eugenics in the United States: "While ostensibly about improv-ing genetic quality, it has been argued that eugenics was more about preserving the position of the dominant groups in the population. Scholarly research has determined that people who found themselves targets of the eugenics movement were those who were seen as unfit for society—the poor, the disabled, the mentally ill, and specific com-munities of color—and a disproportionate number of those who fell victim to eugenicists' sterilization initiatives were women who identi-fied as African American, Hispanic, or Native American. As a result, the United States' Progressive-era eugenics movement is now generally associated with racist and nativist elements, as the movement was to some extent a reaction to demographic and population changes, as well as concerns over the economy and social well-being, rather than scientific genetics." Fortunately, eugenics never really gained a solid stance in the United States because of the moral implications. Who would decide what a "bad" trait was, and how qualified were they to make a decision like that? As Professor Gimbel stated: "The Eugenicists, in trying to remove the suffering that comes from genetic defects, failed to see that people with genetic defects are people; they are defined by their humanity not by their disease."

By the end of the 19th century, there came into being a scientific study of the mind. This study is now called psychology. It was discovered that simply allowing people to talk about their problems relieved a lot of their mental anguish. However, what I found most interesting in the course on this subject is what Professor Gimbel said about Sigmund Freud and Carl Jung. Sigmund Freud said that people should not be looked at individually. They are "internalized relations: relations between the people in our lives, between the parts of our mind, and with events in the past." Those relations are a part of our reality. Carl Jung went even further. He said that there is a part of our mind that contains memories and experiences that are not our own. They are from our ancestors. This is called the collective unconscious. So, our reality is linked to our relationships, but is there a kind of "muscle memory" that our reality is directly influenced by our ancestors? I think so. Here is what Wikipedia says about something called transgenerational trauma: "Transgenerational trauma, or intergenerational trauma is a psychological term which asserts that trauma can be transferred in between generations. After a first generation of survivors experiences trauma, they are able to transfer their trauma to their children and further generations of offspring via complex post-traumatic stress disorder mechanisms. This field of research is relatively young, but has expanded in recent years."

Over the years, psychologists have done a lot of experiments to learn more about the nature of the mind and man. There were a number of experiments done where people were to respond to authority and perform tasks that could ultimately harm other people, and it was found that people could actually hurt others when a person in authority said to do it, and they would take full responsibility for the action. As I found out from Wikipedia, these experiments were called the Milgram experiments conducted by Yale University psychologist Stanley Milgram. Personally, this type of experiment is disturbing, but what is more disturbing to me is that impartial psychologists could actually design these types of experiments that may cause physical or mental harm to any human being.

There were studies done on gender roles as well. It was found that there is a difference between men and women in how they approach relationships. Men tend to approach relationships as a contract between individuals. If you do or give something to me, then I will do or give something to you in return – in other words, a contract where the ruling principle is justice for all parties. Women approach relationships differently. They approach them from a standpoint of caring. They get to know other people's personal needs and try to foster these people's development as a human being. Could we say that men act in a zero sum way and women act in a non-zero sum way? Maybe, and then again, maybe not. Men are not necessarily intolerant of others, but you have to admit there is a certain parallel here.

I'm sure that there were many more types of psychological experiments and studies done over the years, but can we draw a conclusion about the nature of man and ultimately the mind from this limited sampling?

Probably not, but we can still ask: is the nature of man good or evil? This is a black or white question, and I don't think the answer is that simple. The answer is probably in the gray area. We all know people who are good to others and do selfless acts all the time without expecting anything in return. My wife, Helen, is a good example of this type of person. She is constantly helping others who are in need of some sort of help, and she does this selflessly without any expectation of anything in return. My younger daughter, Jennifer, is also a good example. When Jen and I were visiting my older daughter in Mexico, we saw that there were a lot of stray dogs roaming about in the streets, and, yes, she wanted to bring them home with her. While she was living in New York she actually adopted a sick stray dog left out in the cold of New York. While we are talking about daughters and their good qualities, I have to include my older daughter, Angelee, as well. Angelee has always been interested in social justice of some sort. She worked on a hotline for domestic violence after college, and she also received her master's degrees in social work and public health. She is now at Dana Farber Cancer Center as a counselor for cancer patients. God love her! That has to be very draining, especially when a patient passes away.

On the flip side, we all know people who are focused only on themselves and their own needs. They are not evil per se, but they certainly tip the scales in that direction. However, most people on earth are a combination of both – the gray area. I know that I am one of them. I help my family when they need help, and I will always do so. However, I can be selfish. For example, I need to take time to do my studying, reading, and writing every week, and I certainly get cranky when that is disturbed. Oh well, I'm not perfect, even though my wife is constantly trying to "reform" me. In any event, take some time to reflect on what you think the nature of man really is. I'm sure you'll find out something about yourself as well, in the process of doing this reflection.

Professor Gimbel moved on to talk about the brain itself, and its different parts and functions. We won't cover that material, because we already covered it when we discussed Dr. Newberg's analysis of the spiritual brain. However, there is one thing Professor Gimbel mentions in this course that sheds some light on the notion of free will.

Here's a quote from his course: "According to some studies, only 5% of our decisions are caused by conscious attention to situations. The overwhelming majority of our decisions are made by the noncognitive parts of our brains. Our brains decide for us, then we interpret that decision to make it seem to ourselves that we meant it all along."

If you recall, previously I had mentioned that it seems like our brains are constantly seeing and reacting to our environment. Perhaps there is more to it than we think. So, do we have free will? Something to think about.

A particularly interesting part of the course was the discussion on evolutionary psychology. Every human on earth evolved from *Homo sapiens*, which came out of East Africa 250,000 years ago, and every one of us has the same original ancestor. The "biochemist, Allan Wilson, was able to trace the roots of humanity back to a single ancestor, mitochondrial Eve." I think this is particularly interesting from a spiritual perspective. Since we all evolved from the same ancestor, it makes one question why there is so much tension in the world between nations, tribal groups, races, ethnic groups, and even immediate family members. There should not be so much tension between all of our cousins in the world, but there is. For one thing, I suspect it has something to do with the fact that many of our "cousins" live so far away, and secondly because many of them changed physically and don't look like us. We are a species that embraces people who look like us. Why is that? Well, I think it makes us feel safe, for one thing. They look like me, so they can be trusted. If they don't look like me, then I should fear them. If you think about this logically, it does not make sense. There is no basis for this fear. Perhaps this comes from our original survival instincts. If I want to survive, I need to be aware of my surroundings and be aware of dangers that are lurking around the corner. Perhaps as a species we haven't evolved that far yet; otherwise we might embrace others more willingly. Yes, we need to be aware of dangers, but perhaps we can extend an olive branch to others first and go from there. Yes, this is hard to do, but if we want to advance as a civilized society, we will have to find a way of doing both: protecting ourselves and opening up to others at the same time. What do you think?

Professor Gimbel points out that, for 238,000 of the last 250,000 years, our ancestors lived the same Stone Age life of hunting and foraging in small groups. It has only been within the last 12,000 years that we saw a great leap in the development of man with the development of agriculture, metallurgy, antibiotics, etc. In evolutionary terms alone, it should have taken a great deal more time to see the advancements we have seen in the last 12,000 years. Why such a great increase in such a short time? It is speculated that for the previous 238,000 years the brains of our ancestors were going through a great amount of neurological changes to adapt to the environment and that, in the process, it was setting the stage for the brains and minds of our ancestors to break out and find the full potential of what humans can do. As a result, little by little over the last 12,000 years, man developed the tools and knowledge not only to survive but to succeed and grow as a species. For example, man developed the ability to read expressions on faces to determine if someone might be friend or foe. Man as a whole also developed a sense of altruism somewhere along the line. Yes, we see that if man is put in the wrong situation, he can cause harm to others, but is it an exceptional part of life? I believe we are not generally put into those situations, and when we are, we may be very uncomfortable with the situation. Is it because of an inherited altruistic nature? Again, we ask: Is the nature of man good or bad or something in the gray area? There are naturally bad people in the world as well, but again, I think that may be the exception and not the rule. Would man as a whole have developed some sense of altruism if he had bad tendencies? I think not. Therefore, I think the nature of man is tipping toward the good side, where probably most of us are in the gray area. What do you think?

Additionally, there is a part of evolutionary psychology called ecopsychology where the development of man is not just about looking out for number one. Again, can we ask: Is this part of an altruistic nature that evolved, or a matter of survival? In this case, I think it is a matter of survival. Man developed as a part of an entire ecosystem. Man is dependent on his environment and all the living plants, animals, streams, etc. to help him survive in this world. He is not just a single being. He is just one part of the natural world, and it would behoove him to make sure he takes care of his precious planet. This might explain why we generally relax when we are out in nature. It is part of our evolution. Could this be linked to our "muscle memory" of our ancestors' experiences? I think there may be something to it.

Professor Gimbel moves on to sociology, where the individual is not the only part to his or her reality. Every individual is just one factor within their group or society. This is also their reality as well. I guess you could say that there are layers to our reality. We all have to adjust to our own feelings and thoughts, but that isn't the only thing. We have to be in tune to our environment for all of our survival, and additionally, we have to be aware of the people and rules that govern our society. This view is called the emergence view where reality has different levels—or layers, as I like to say. So, societies play an important role in our reality. For example, you could call a sports team a society of sorts. If you are a member of a sports team you will certainly have to behave according to the team rules and not do what you want to do in all cases. The team will exist, whether or not you are a member of it. You must go to practices, team meetings, work out in the gym, etc. If you don't, you will be excluded from the privilege of being a member of it. This is an example of a society that is working toward the collective good of not just the team but the individuals as well. However, if you don't like it, you can always leave. No harm done either way. Societies, for the most part, are good for the individuals. Let's take governments, for example. Most governments provide rules, regulations, and laws for the good of everyone, but societies need to be policed to make sure they don't harm their members. In all societies, there are consequences if the rules are not followed. An example of a harmful society was seen in the late 1880s in Europe. Suicides increased greatly in the Protestant population. Why was this? Well, Protestant society at that time was very restrictive. Everyone had to think, act, and even feel according to the norms of that society. As a result, many were so pressured because of their inability or desire to conform that many ended up taking their own lives. Catholics, on the other hand, did not have the same constraints, and their society was more comforting to their individuals. Familial relationships were an important part of Catholic society. Protestants, on the other hand, did not have this comfort level in their society at the time. So, we see this as an example of a society run amok. How can societies police themselves so this does not happen? Surprisingly enough, it is the criminals in societies that provide the policing. Criminals push the boundaries of society and if there is enough push by enough people, things in the society will eventually change. Think back to the Revolutionary War in the United States. Our forefathers were considered criminals by the British at the time. People like George Washington, John Adams, and Thomas Jefferson were criminals to the British. Yet today, we in the US see them as brave heroes. These criminals created a positive change in our society at the time. Yes, it is strange, but societies need criminals to police and make positive change in our societies. However, there are different types of criminals. There are criminals like George Washington who effect a positive change, and then there are criminals like serial killers who provide nothing but harm to our societies. We need to be clear on this point. There are really bad people who exist, and they need to be controlled and separated from our society.

Societies also need a healthy amount of competition and cooperation to thrive. For example, people need to compete with one another to keep the price of goods down to an affordable level for everyone. Additionally, there needs to be cooperation between everyone to help the less fortunate in the societal group. Societies need racial diversity as well. We all live in this world together, and in my opinion, different races will help keep a balance of individual needs, wants, and desires for a society to function effectively. However, societies need to make sure that no one individual is negatively singled out because of his or her differences. This is an area that all too often leads to disruption in a society if diversity is not embraced.

Professor Gimbel made a point that many societies and the great civilizations of the past have collapsed. "The American anthropologist Joseph Tainter concluded that the Roman Empire, the Egyptian Old Kingdom, the Mayan civilization, and others all sputtered and died from a lack of energy." Societies create social structures or institutions to take care of problems, needs, or threats. These institutions generate a need for resources to solve problems, and that puts a certain stress on the society as a whole. Bureaucracies take care of solving the problems, but at a cost for everyone. As the complexity of bureaucracies increase, it is found that society has intertwined layers of institutions all competing for limited resources. Eventually, the society or civilization collapses under its own bureaucratic weight from a lack of energy to handle all of the problems created by its complex structure. This kind of makes you wonder about our own society. We certainly live in a very bureaucratic society here in the United States. So, will it collapse sometime? If so, when? Is this our social reality? Something to think about, at any rate.

The professor moves on and describes many other realities for us. One such reality is that, for many years, it was always thought that for life to evolve and thrive on earth, sunlight energy was an essential requirement. However in 1977, researchers from Woods Hole Oceanographic Institution here in Massachusetts discovered that life was thriving in the deep sea at the Galapagos Rift in the Pacific Ocean, a mile and a half under the sea where there was very hot magna from cracks in the earth's crust. There was abundant life here with no sunlight, and this life did not depend on photosynthesis from the sun. Instead there was chemosynthesis from the heat and chemical energy coming out of the thermal vents on the ocean floor. This makes one wonder about our origins. Did we evolve from photosynthesis, chemosynthesis, or perhaps both?

Another reality is that fairly recently, scientists discovered that there are about twenty-one planets orbiting other suns that appear able to sustain life. Even if there is life on these planets, there is no way of telling whether that life would be basic organisms or more evolved life forms. Will we ever discover their existence? I don't think it will be anytime soon, with our limited technology, but we need to keep on exploring.

Yet another reality is the advances that have been and are being made that could eventually have an impact for humans. New drugs and medical procedures are just starting to increase life expectancy for humans. Cloning of animals has been done, but it has produced major genetic flaws and diseases which certainly raises ethical questions about continuing in this direction. In the late 20th century, genetic engineering came into being and promises some useful advancements at changing organisms and plants, such as growing bigger and better crops for our consumption. Again, what will the long-term effects be for us after consuming this food? Could it alter our biological functions in some way for the worse? I'm sure we will find out. There are also new discoveries in the area of drugs. There are drugs that can make us run faster, lift heavier objects, have quicker reactions, etc. What are the long-term effects of their use? We are finding out now. Steroids, for example, have been found to cause certain illnesses and "roid rage" after long-term use. Lastly, there have been great leaps in the development of prosthetics for people missing arms or legs. In the last twenty years or so, it is clear that these new prosthetics have made life easier for some people. There is no way to replace an actual limb, but some prosthetics have allowed a lot of people the ability to function almost as well as they did in the past. It makes one wonder whether there will be a time when these prosthetics will greatly exceed the capabilities of human limbs. Actually, I think we are there in some instances based on some of the recent news articles. Move over, Iron Man.

Professor Gimbel also describes the advances in Artificial Intelligence and where it might go in the future, but we have covered that already in the philosophy section, so I won't rehash that again. However, he moves on to a new concept that I never thought about before – the value of information. He states: "In 1948, Norbert Wiener published the book *Cybernetics: Or, Control and Communication in the Animal and Machine.* The central insight of the book is that information, rather than energy, is the central notion in all of science." Hmmmmm.... Well, it is generally thought that " 'Doing science' meant finding the equations that govern energy transfer in particular systems and showing how energy creates work, light, order and life." Norbert suggested that we reframe the commonalities of all science to focus on information rather than energy. He reasons that cause and effect is the basic notion underlying all of science.

For example: Is quantum mechanics all about information of some sort? Remember the quantum entanglement issue?

Earlier it was stated: "...if one connected subatomic particle is doing 'something' at one end of the galaxy, the other connected particle mimics its action at the other end of the galaxy in the opposite direction. Distance does not seem to matter here. If you think about it, we said that nothing can go faster than the speed of light, yet somehow the actions of a particle a great distance away seems to influence another particle at the same time, though even the speed of light could not reach the other particle to provide this instantaneous reaction." This is about some sort of communication between these distant particles—or information being passed, if you will. This kind of makes you think, doesn't it?

Another example is evolution. Genetic information is transferred to offspring. Additionally, the science of psychology is about communicating information between participants to help someone with psychological issues.

These examples may not be the best examples, but I think they help you get the idea that information is not only important to science but to our reality as well.

Professor Gimbel then moves on to explain how the internet is a wealth of information that can be used to affect our reality. The internet can help us learn about new things that we never knew before to help us with our jobs, schoolwork, etc. However, we have to be careful, because the internet provides sites that can be one-sided and draw in those people with similar views. This could be harmless depending on the view, but it could be dangerous if the view could be destructive to people outside of the group.

Virtual Reality is another form of information. It provides us with an escape to enter a new kind of reality, or a world that is outside of our usual environment. In virtual reality games, we enter a new place from our everyday world to do things that we cannot normally do, and play interesting games. These games are a form of reality, but only for a short period of time until we need to eat, go to work, etc. in our physical world.

Next, Professor Gimbel talks about Data Analytics. In my simple way, I define data analytics as the collection of information on certain behaviors of people and then extrapolating from that information what the behavior of those people will be in the future. For example, grocery stores, department stores, etc. track the purchases of individuals and then use this information to best figure out what their next purchase might be and then send them a coupon or some other enticement to purchase that next item.

So you can see that information is a very important part of our reality, right from quantum mechanics, through our evolution, through our genetic make-up, through our use of the internet, through our game-playing, and through our future purchases for our dinner tonight.

Lastly, Professor Gimbel summarizes the key points of the course:

Basically, our reality is very complex. First, there is the reality that we see in objects and the object's interactions with the rest of what we see. It's a very individual view of reality from our own mind's eye. Secondly, there is the reality we experience with our neighbors, family, and friends or our small social groups whom we must co-exist with daily. Lastly, there is the much larger reality of co-existence that we live in a whole world and universe with governments, rules, and regulations both from man and the laws of science for our behavior in this world and the universe as a whole.

So, what can we say about reality? Well, we are not alone. It is not just about us. Our reality involves everything that is happening in the universe, and we need to accept it, good or bad.

There was a bunch of good information to think about from this course, and I apologize for packing so much in the last few pages, but I think you would agree that it was very interesting. I really recommend that you take this course to get a better understanding of your place in this great universe, if you want to learn more.

SUMMARY

*W*ell, I am at the end of my studies. So, what do I do now? First, how about a summary of sorts of the key takeaway points from this endeavor? After that, I think it will be time to draw some conclusions.

From the book *The Evolution of God* by Robert Wright, the first thing we see is what the early humans believed about a God. It appears that in early human development, most gods met the immediate needs of the various people and their rulers, such as: safe childbirth, a good season of crops, safe travel to the next town, etc.

The book was primarily written about the Abrahamic religions of Judaism, Christianity, and Islam and provided a lot of information about their beliefs and central figures, which I'm not going to mention again here. However, there was an interesting theme throughout the book. Are the religions and/or beliefs of the people of the world zero sum or non-zero sum? To review:

Zero sum: implies an intolerance to other people's gods and beliefs

Non-zero sum: implies a tolerance to other people's gods and beliefs, whether or not it is for political or economic stability or gain.

We can think of certain religions and beliefs that provide an example of each, but the main point is that there is a little of each in the world. I don't think we can say we are headed one way or the other when it comes to tolerance. There are so many different types of people in the world who are influenced by their religions and environments in good and bad ways to the point that we cannot predict their level of tolerance for others. In terms of human nature, this is neither good nor bad. It just is what it is.

However, I personally believe everyone should be tolerant of others. That is just me, and there is the following quote from the book that I think sums up what I took from this book.

Ashoka, an Indian Emperor (268 -232 BCE) who was a Buddhist, said, "If man extols his own faith and disparages another because of devotion to his own and because he wants to glorify it, he seriously injures his own faith."

After my reading of Robert Wright's book, I moved on to the world's religions from the various courses and internet study. I will not "rehash" any of that material, but I think it is worth restating my thoughts.

We saw how the ancient Jewish God was a jealous God and required excessive rituals of obedience. He chose the Jewish people as his people. He wanted them to have no other gods. Exactly why were they the chosen ones? Were they better than other people? Or is it that it is human nature to want to be special, and the early Jews just declared that God liked them the best? However, we see this in Christianity and Islam as well, where those religions professed that their 'Way' was the best. We see this tendency in other religions as well. In Hinduism and

Buddhism, we see that they don't reject other people because they believe differently, but they believe what they want to believe and practice their own rituals, because to them it provides the 'Way' for them. I believe we can conclude that whatever religion a man follows, it is solely a personal choice for him and him alone. He makes his choices based on what makes him feel comfortable. Everyone is certainly influenced by their environment and the religions and beliefs of their parents, but ultimately man needs to feel comfortable and he may often change his perceptions of his local religious world view to suit his personal needs.

We saw that at first gods were for the benefit of man in his daily life – good crops, safe trips to the next town, successful childbirths, etc. Later, we saw that man was not just satisfied with help in his everyday life from the gods. He wanted more. He saw himself as an individual person and started to wonder about his existence and place in the universe. It was then that he started to explore in the recesses of his mind his own meaning in life and ask some very tough questions. What would happen to him? Where would he go when he dies? Is there a heaven? If so, then if he is morally good will it help him to get to heaven? If there is a heaven, what is it like? If there isn't a heaven, then what happens? Does his life and his soul end at death and his existence as an individual end? Does God really exist?

These are some very deep and important questions that mankind has asked and still is asking himself. Quite frankly, the answers to these questions are rooted in faith and not in truth. We found that out in our study of philosophy, which provides a great deal of insight regarding our reality. Again, I'm not going to restate the specifics of that study. Instead, I will just say that after my study of philosophy, which is the study devoted to finding out the truth in our universe, that there is no proof that the soul, free will, mind, and God or gods exist. Here are my thoughts.

Even though there is no proof that a God or gods exist, there is also no proof that they don't. If you are religious, you just have to make that leap and believe whatever you feel comfortable within the framework of your own spiritual and religious beliefs. As an observation, I believe that most religions are good. Most religions provide stories for good moral behavior and seem to teach their people the right way to act and behave in a moral and just society. This is a good thing, and I think that religions provide a good social fabric for people to get along and live together in peace whether or not they believe in God or ultimately whether there is a God or not.

Next, I moved on to what current-day science can tell us about the reality of the universe that we all live in now. There was a lot of material in the science sections that was new to me but very enlightening. Some of the material was very difficult to imagine, but it is what it is. Again, here are my thoughts.

There are a great many things science has told us that are hard to understand. Nothing can go faster than the speed of light. Time slows down the faster you are going. Gravity is actually the 'bending' of the spacetime continuum. Black Holes are really scary strong forces of gravity. The interaction of the subatomic particles of the standard model of particle physics is very complex. Additionally, science has also proposed a lot of theories, thoughts, and questions about the universe, as well. Do multiple dimensions exist? Do multiple universes exist? Why does quantum entanglement exist? Will the universe stop expanding and collapse in on itself? Why do dark matter and dark energy exist, if in fact they really do exist?

We could go on listing the things that we know and do not know, but suffice it to say that there just is so much more to learn about our world and that it may be endless. In the meantime, we just need to accept our place in this world and be in awe of its magnificence.

That's what I learned from my study of science, but the last sentence above summarizes my feeling about the universe. It is grand and perhaps unknowable, and we need to be in awe of it and the small place we occupy in it. Don't you agree?

Suppose for a moment that God or the universe let us in on some of the deeper secrets—would man have the ability to grasp and comprehend them and their meaning? Remember, the Jains believed the limitations of human knowledge to what we hold as true are only tentative. This principle of "non-absolutism" means that we may be wrong about what we hold as true. The Daoists believed that there are two aspects of Dao, which is the way of nature: one that can be talked about and one that cannot be talked about, so the human understanding of the Dao is limited. Lastly, in the Baha'i faith it is said that humans cannot completely know God because God is greater than the whole, and therefore we will not know the complete truth. Do these religions know that what man can possibly comprehend is limited? Perhaps, but the point is that man by his nature has limitations, and we should recognize that and embrace it as a truth. I do not mean that we should not stop trying to learn more about our universe. However, we need to accept and embrace the fact that we may never know all its secrets.

I have a spiritual question to consider. If multiple dimensions and universes exist, could there be some that are on a vastly bigger scale than our own environment, such that we would appear as a tiny speck from their frame of reference? If so, doesn't that make you feel small? Likewise, perhaps there are some that are on a vastly smaller scale as well. Perhaps, there are an infinite number of them and our environment is somewhere in the middle. In any event, if they exist, then we are just a very small part of the picture.

Lastly, I revisited what reality is, from our study of philosophy, because let's face it, what we see, feel, hear, taste, and smell are the only avenues into actually knowing what the reality of the universe is and this influences our sense of spirituality. But I found out that our reality is so much more than what our own senses tell us.

Basically, our reality is very complex. First, there is the reality that we see in objects and the object's interactions with the rest of what we see. It's a very individual view of reality from our own mind's eye. Secondly, there is the reality we experience with our neighbors, family, and friends or our small social groups whom we must co-exist with daily. Lastly, there is the much larger reality of co-existence that we live in a whole world and universe with governments, rules, and regulations both from man and the laws of science for our behavior in this world and the universe as a whole.

So, what can we say about reality? Well, we are not alone. It is not just about us. Our reality involves everything that is happening in the universe and we need to accept it, good or bad.

In any event, I think that this short summary adequately encapsulates my spiritual journey through religion, philosophy, science, and reality. So, where is this ordinary man now? What conclusions can I draw about my beliefs and my place in this universe?

I need to draw conclusions, so let's go!

DRAWING CONCLUSIONS

First, let's revisit philosophy once more. In David Kyle Johnson's course, you could understand completely that in addressing the big questions of philosophy, he was on a quest to point us in the direction of gaining wisdom through the process of finding the truth, the complete truth, no matter what it was. The philosophy of religion course gave me a different kind of feeling. James Hall made this statement about the course: "It is simply philosophy of religion which examines religion from a philosophical point of view trying to gain wisdom, truth, and knowledge." He used this approach to examine the existence of God. There are three kinds of arguments for the existence of God that Professor Hall provided: the ontological, the cosmological, and the teleological arguments. I will not repeat them here, because you can review them again for yourself in that section, but if you recall, I really didn't give them much weight in terms of providing any real proof regarding the existence of God, so even though Professor Hall was on the quest for wisdom, truth, and knowledge, as David Kyle Johnson was, I came away feeling that the truth about God was at best elusive. I think that Professor Hall probably felt the same way, because he went on to explain the real motivation for the theists and religious of the world. Proof that God exists is not relevant to their faiths. They simply take 'a leap of faith' and frame their world around this leap of faith. Since they are completely invested in their world view, it can be hard for them to see another point of view. This view of the world may or may not be the way the world actually is, but that doesn't matter. They are comfortable with how they see it. So, even though the philosophy of religion is a quest for the truth, I think we can say that it really is about faith.

There is a term for this – relativism – which basically means that truth is relative to each individual. They believe that what they believe is the truth. Personally, I like to have evidence, probably because of my analytical nature. However, does that mean I don't have faith? Well, I'm going to explore that a bit more as we go along. I've come to find out that I am a much more complex ordinary man than I ever thought.

Let's move on now. Overall, I feel that I left the matter of the existence of the soul, free will, and the mind somewhat hanging, at least from my perspective. Philosophy says that there is no proof of their existence, as it says the same thing about God. However, those three are very personal to each and every one of us. How can we say they don't exist? We all seem to think they are our essence, or at least it appears that way to us. Are we all being fooled? We think, so we must have a mind. Right! We can choose to eat a hamburger instead of a piece of celery, so we must have free will. We can choose to do right or wrong, which seems to be the essence of our souls. In the course on redefining reality, it was said:

"According to some studies, only 5% of our decisions are caused by conscious attention to situations. The overwhelming majority of our decisions are made by the noncognitive parts of our brains. Our brains decide for us, then we interpret that decision to make it seem to ourselves that we meant it all along."

Hmmmmmm…. So, let's think about this area a bit more. If the soul, free will, and our minds don't exist, then where does our spirituality come from? Can our spirituality just be a fabrication created by the biology and chemistry of our brains? Personally, I would like to think that it is not the case. I think, therefore I am; so I must have a mind. Right! I also think that I make my own decisions for myself. I would much prefer to have that hamburger with cheese and pickles instead of a piece of celery. Additionally, I have a sense of what is right to do, such as we have to take care of people that are less fortunate than we are by helping them with food and housing. Our contributions to charities and churches help us to do it. It feels right. We help our families when they are down and out. It feels right. So, how can our spiritually be a fabrication created by our brains, either whole or in part? As I said above, I would like to think that is not the case. However, the door to doubt is left open. What do I believe? Does it all come down to a matter of faith? And what is faith, exactly? Does my brain's biology and chemistry churn away and leave me with a reality one way or the other? Does it leave me believing that I have a mind, soul, free will, and a belief in God? Does it leave me having faith in the existence of those essential elements of what it means to be human? Well, quite frankly, I will never know the answer to those questions, and neither will you. Our existence will always be a mystery, and that is probably the way it should be. A lot of the laws of the universe will remain hidden to us. I'm okay with that! It is what it is, and there is nothing that can be done other than to accept it.

So, where does that leave me spiritually? Whether or not our "essence" is a fabrication of our brains, I still exist and think, so I still need to continue to explore my "essence" no matter where it comes from. What do

I believe or not believe? Quite frankly, I need to continue because only that effort will lead me to a certain level of comfort with myself and what I believe, and that is all I can expect spiritually. I need to be comfortable in my "mind" about my place in the universe. When I do that, then I will have found my place spiritually…but more on that later.

Continuing on…throughout my study, I have grappled with the question: Is the nature of man good or bad? I came to the conclusion, which I still believe to be true, that the nature of man is neither good nor bad. Man's nature is basically in the gray area. I think we all have seen this in ourselves. Throughout our lives, we can point to some things we did that were really helpful, and then again we can find examples of things that make us ashamed of ourselves. Yet, I want to believe that in some small way, the nature of man is tipping toward the good.

In the first part of this century, at my place of work, I was responsible for the IT part of the conversion of our company's client systems from an IBM to an UNIX operating system for cost efficiency. As part of this effort, I was given a number of programmers to facilitate this endeavor over the course of several years. The majority of this programming effort came from South Africa. I eventually learned a bit about South Africa. As you may know, South Africa was in a state of apartheid for many years until the unjust society fell apart under its own weight and free elections were given to all in the 1990s. However, there was an occurrence that showed the nature of man leaning toward the good at a very large scale. South Africa set up the Truth and Reconciliation Commission to find justice, reconciliation, and forgiveness for the atrocities that occurred during apartheid.

As Wikipedia states at:

https://en.wikipedia.org/wiki/Truth_and_Reconciliation_Commission_(South_Africa)

"The Truth and Reconciliation Commission (TRC) was a court-like restorative justice body assembled in South Africa after the end of apartheid. Witnesses who were identified as victims of gross human rights violations were invited to give statements about their experiences, and some were selected for public hearings. Perpetrators of violence could also give testimony and request amnesty from both civil and criminal prosecution.

The TRC, the first of the 1003 held internationally to stage public hearings, was seen by many as a crucial component of the transition to full and free democracy in South Africa. Despite some flaws, it is generally (although not universally) thought to have been successful.

....

The TRC's emphasis on reconciliation was in sharp contrast to the approach taken by the Nuremberg Trials and other de-Nazification measures. The reconciliatory approach was seen as a successful way of dealing with human-rights violations after political change, either from internal or external factors. Consequently, other countries have instituted similar commissions, though not always with the same scope or the allowance for charging those currently in power..."

Anyway, I found out that there were many examples of victims forgiving their perpetrators in South Africa during this process. They did not forget what happened to them, but they had the courage to forgive. Just think about how hard it would be to face your perpetrator, accept their apology, and then move on. Would I have the strength to do that?

I would like to think I would, but I just don't know. All I can say is that as nation, these people had great courage and strength which truly shows that the nature of man, in this case, is leaning toward the good.

'The chair of the Truth & Reconciliation Commission (TRC), Archbishop Tutu, has said that "there can be no future without forgiveness."' – from https://law.pepperdine.edu/straus/training-and-conferences/forgiveness-reconciliation-healing.htm

I want to believe that there are occurrences all around the world like this one, nudging the nature of man toward the good end of the scale, even though there are probably as many events nudging it the other way. I guess you could say that I have faith in man, whether or not it is completely justified. Faith is a powerful part of the universe, is it not?

Alright! The next thing I want to do is address the elephant in the room. Why on earth did I spend the last few years studying, taking a number of courses, reading, and writing about religions, God, and spirituality? I bet you are thinking, is Jim afraid to die? Well, unfortunately for you, if you thought that, and fortunately for me, I can say that it is not the case. The fear of death is certainly a factor that I'm sure everyone considers when they think about their place in the universe. It is natural. No one really wants to die. It is a big unknown, and everyone is fearful of the unknown. Does our "essence" continue on in some way, or is that the end and we are no more? We just don't know. However, the concept of death is fascinating. Yes, I said fascinating. Think about it. No one knows what it is like to die. There hasn't been anyone who came back to tell any of us what it was like after they were gone for a number of years and gave us an update. No one came back and said that every day was sunny. You could eat ice cream day and night and not gain weight. You and your friends looked twenty years old again. You could fly around all day without effort all over heaven to visit your friends. Right! That sounds great, but there has been no one to tell us what it really is like.

Previously, I mentioned that perhaps emergency rooms could put images and words on the tops of the cabinets that could not be seen from the floor, and then if a near-death occurrence happened, the staff could ask that person if they saw anything. If they were able to restate the words and describe the images, then that would certainly get my attention. However, as I have said before, I am skeptical. Can we take the testimony of someone else as the truth? Personally, I would be skeptical even if someone else verified it. I guess I am a man of reason, and I would probably believe it only if it were my personal experience. Additionally, in a situation like this, we have to also consider that the person may be dying but perhaps not quite dead yet, even if the medical instruments say it is so. Could it be that the brain is rapidly firing its neurons and the person is experiencing, seeing, and hearing things from their past memory, so that when or if they return to life, they can report it? Perhaps. However, if the person describes the words and images on the cabinets.... Well, that cannot be explained as a few neurons firing off while they are lying on the table. So, are you skeptical, or do you have faith?

Yes, death is fascinating from an intellectual point of view, but it is a very personal experience, and we can only hope that it is painless and pleasant. We all will die someday. We can't dwell on it. It will happen, and it is what it is.

So, why then did I spend the last several years at this endeavor? Why am I spiritual? My only defense is that I can only say that I am a spiritual being... but why? I have always been a pensive individual. I am always thinking about something, and perhaps that leads me to explore what I don't know.

One definition of spiritual is: "relating to or affecting the human spirit or soul as opposed to material or physical things."

There's that word again – soul. I guess I'm interested in exploring the essence of my being. Well, that seems somewhat logical, because for some reason I have never been interested in acquiring material things, so if I'm going to be thinking about things, it seems logical that I might spend some time thinking about my place and everyone else's place in this universe.

When I was young, I never thought of myself as spiritual. In my high school and college years, it seems that all I was interested in was developing a career and finding my place in this material world. I chose mathematics as a major in college and figured it would be a help in getting a job. Due to the influence of my mother, I also pointed myself in the direction of serving in the military. I went to a military college, Norwich University, in Vermont, and then I joined the US Army as a lieutenant in the infantry, where I served for four years of active duty. This certainly does not sound to me like the path of a spiritual person. Perhaps in my early years I was not as pensive as I thought.

However, my sister gave me a book. The book was *The True Solitude* by Thomas Merton. He was a Trappist monk who wrote in his early years about matters of a spiritual nature, and then later on about issues that weighed on his mind such as war, racial injustice, and the increasing violence in American life.

My sister put the following inscription on the cover page.

"I have seen that you find a peculiar comfort in both solitude and God. So keep this book with you, read it, and be comforted.

For Jimmy on his 19th birthday from Earlene."

I am surprised that this book made it through the last 46 years without getting lost or thrown away. I recently found it with some old stuff of mine.

When I turned nineteen, I had just completed my first year at Norwich University. As many of you may know, the first year at a military college can be one of the most trying experiences one can have, and one of the most character-building experiences as well. In my own way, I looked to God to help me through. I used the weekly church service to give me a bit of solitude away from the hectic pace of life as a freshman in a military college. Perhaps my sister saw that in me and thought that the book was what I needed.

As I went on in life, I was focused on my career, but there would be times I would think about things that were not material. When I was close to retirement, I decided that I would do this journey, and I am very glad I did, because it not only gave me a purpose and something to do in my retirement, but it also allowed me to explore my "essence" and to think about the nature of the universe.

As I asked above, why am I spiritual? The answer is: I just am. It is my essence.

Now we get to the nitty-gritty. What do I believe? I need to end my study and state my spiritual beliefs at this time in my life. Please be aware that what I believe has no bearing on what you believe. As you have read through to this point, I hope you have gone through your own spiritual journey as well, either agreeing or disagreeing with my thoughts and in the process started to find your own essence. We are all different and will more than likely believe different things. That's a good thing. I certainly wouldn't want a society where people are cookie cutters, all coming from the same mold.

So, what do I believe?

I would like to start by telling you what I believed before I entered into this journey. I kind of believed that God was a sort of duality. I believed that God was an anthropomorphic God in the image of man. As we saw, a lot of people and religions would make their gods into the image of themselves in some way. I think this is normal. A God that looks like us gives us a certain comfort. Secondly, I believed God could transform into a spirit that permeated throughout the universe to help all the creatures in it. To be honest, I never really gave any critical thought as to why I believed this. I just believed that God was there for us and made good decisions to benefit us all.

In 2012, I was feeling a disconnect spiritually from my family. My wife and daughters were Catholic, and I was Protestant. I felt left out of their religious environment, so I started to seriously explore converting to the Catholic faith. Since my spirituality is very important to me, I didn't take this lightly at all. I would think about it all the time. After going to church many times with my family, I had a revelation. I realized that the Catholic Church emphasized the Holy Trinity of the Father, Son, and Holy Spirit to a very large degree. They were all consubstantial. All one and the same. This aligned with my belief of God in the image of man but also a spirit. The only part I had to think about was the son, Jesus, as God. However, this was not hard to accept, because in a way it aligned with a new belief that I was recently turning over in my mind. I was realizing that all creatures are a little part of God, so God was more than a spirit in the image of man. I was realizing that God was also in all of us. I don't know where this belief came from, but I fully embraced it, and when I did, I realized that the Holy Trinity was what I believed wholeheartedly. This was just what I needed. I then made my first Catholic confession in December of 2012, and I fully converted to the Catholic faith and was confirmed in April of 2013.

After I converted, I often wondered whether the scholars of the Catholic Church knew that God was everywhere and in all of his creatures, and that's why they put an emphasis on the Holy Trinity. Perhaps they knew the faithful would accept the Father, Son, and Holy Spirit much more easily than they would accept that God is everywhere and in all creatures. I don't know, but this solidified my faith and allowed me to convert.

Anyway, this is where I was spiritually when I started this journey back in 2016, and I think it was a good starting point.

So, what do I believe now?

Philosophy and science opened my eyes to the universe and what we know—and more importantly, what we don't know.

Philosophy showed me that there is no proof that the soul, free will, the mind and yes God exists. However, it didn't prove to me that they don't exist, either.

Science showed me the wonder of the universe:

There are a great many things science has told us that are hard to understand. Nothing can go faster than the speed of light. Time slows down the faster you are going. Gravity is actually the 'bending' of the space-time continuum. Black Holes are really scary strong forces of gravity.

The interaction of the subatomic particles of the standard model of particle physics is very complex. Additionally, science has also proposed a lot of theories, thoughts, and questions about the universe as well. Do multiple dimensions exist? Do multiple universes exist? Why does quantum entanglement exist? Will the universe stop expanding and collapse in on itself? Why does dark matter and dark energy exist if in fact they really do exist?

Science has showed me just how little we know and probably will ever know about our universe. It certainly has not shown me any proof that god exists or doesn't exist. It has shown me that there are many more questions than answers to our understanding of this great universe. As I have said before, perhaps that's the way it should be. That's okay with me. That's just part of life as a human. We will never know.

I found the following on Wikipedia.

'Robert Jastrow (September 7, 1925 – February 8, 2008) was an American astronomer and planetary physicist. He was a NASA scientist, populist author and futurist....

His expressed views on creation were that although he was an "agnostic, and not a believer", it seems to him that "the curtain drawn over the mystery of creation will never be raised by human efforts, at least in the foreseeable future" due to "the circumstances of the Big Bang-the fiery holocaust that destroyed the record of the past". With the discovery of the Big Bang, Jastrow began to hold a belief that, if there was a beginning to the universe, there was also a Creator.

In an interview with Christianity Today, Jastrow said "Astronomers now find they have painted themselves into a corner because they have proven, by their own methods, that the world began abruptly in an act of creation to which you can trace the seeds of every star, every planet, every living thing in this cosmos and on the earth. And they have found that all this happened as a product of forces they cannot hope to discover. That there are what I or anyone would call supernatural forces at work is now, I think, a scientifically proven fact."'

This is probably about as close as one can get to having a scientific non-believer proclaiming that there has to be a God.

In any event, there is still no proof that God exists, but there is a crack in the doorway. What do you believe? Do you have faith?

Humorously, I think about the Big Bang being started by a little boy in another alternate universe with a firecracker that he sets off... and Bang!.... Our universe was started, billions of years ago.... I kind of wonder how many of those firecrackers he has in his pocket.

The study of philosophy and science has just shown me that there is no proof that exists for the wonders of the world and universe we live in.... but is that really what I want to believe?

Aha! That is the real question that I have to answer, in light of my journey.

What is it that I want to believe?

After undergoing this journey, could it be that God is all the energy and matter in the universe, as well as all the laws that govern everything that happens. $E=mc^2$...energy is matter and matter is energy, nothing can go faster than the speed of light, time slows down the faster you go as well, as all the other laws of the universe dictate what can or cannot happen here. Energy, matter, and the laws of the universe – is this God? When we die, there has to be a release of energy from our bodies.

This energy must be released into the universe around us. Does it go into making other living beings in some way? Or into other forms of matter? Can we call this reincarnation if this is what actually happens? Perhaps the Hindus and Buddhists are on to something here.

Energy, matter, and laws – are they an intelligent design that has purpose, knowledge, ability, and a will to control everything here? By our observation, we cannot tell if there is any intelligence to everything that happens in the universe. This is likely because man by his nature is limited in whatever he can know.

Remember in our science study we saw our limitations in making measurements as it relates to the "particles" of the universe. If you used photons or 'particles' of light to 'observe' an electron's velocity and position the photon's contact with the electron will actually alter the electron's velocity or position or perhaps both. This statement may not be completely scientifically correct, but it really does make the point that we humans may be limited in what we can ever know or at least know at this time in scientific history which certainly adds to the mystic of this great universe.

There may be an infinite number of things to be learned about the universe. If so, man's knowledge is definitely limited by his nature. I'm okay with this. God is unknowable.

However, am I okay with the image of God as the energy, matter, and laws of the universe that appear to interact by cause and effect with or without some intelligent design to it? Not really. This image of God seems to be rather impersonal to this ordinary man. Yet, this could be God. Should I believe this?

Again, what do I want to believe?

The answer is that I believe what I want to believe. I believe God exists despite the evidence to the contrary. I believe that God is unknowable, kind, caring, all knowing, forgiving, generous, and all present to everyone and everything. I believe this because I have faith. Yes, I will say it again. I have faith that God exists. After all this study and the many scholars that seem to point to the fact that there is no proof of God's existence, I still believe. As I have said many times before, people need to feel comfortable not only in their physical lives but in their spiritual beliefs. I am a man of reason, so why do I now go against all the reasoning that I went through in this study that I made over the last several years? Well, the answer is not simple. It is because I am a very complex ordinary man. This ordinary man needs to feel comfortable with his beliefs, and now I do.

I believe that God doesn't subscribe to any one religion. He adapts himself or herself to each and every one of us, and God takes the form that each of us subscribes to him or her, whether or not God is in human form.

Why does God do this? Well, God comes to life from each and every one of our imaginations. He works hard to adapt himself to us personally and individually. He works very hard for everyone so that we feel comfortable with our individual relationships. That is God, and God does it for all of us, because God is love. We are all a little part of God.

God is my wife, daughters, granddaughters, and every one of you. We all have our bad and cranky sides, but in each and every one of us is God, and that is why we love.

Well, that is what I believe. There is no reason to, but I believe it. I am comfortable with my ordinary spiritual existence.

When I started this journey, I had only a few questions that I wanted to explore. However, as I went on, you can see that I found many more questions along the way than answers. It's funny, but I'm okay with not finding the answers to my many questions. We are simply human, and there will always be questions that we cannot possibly answer. It just is the nature of being human.

So, now that I have finished my research work, does that mean my spiritual journey has come to an end? I think not. You see. I believe that every human being is capable of growing spiritually right until the end when we die. Every day we have new experiences and thoughts. This adds to who we are as humans. No one can possibly tell each one of us how these experiences and thoughts will cause us to grow spiritually. Some people may only inch along in their spiritual growth while others may take leaps and bounds. All of us are different and will grow spiritually at different rates, and that is okay. The key is that we all grow spiritually and are comfortable with that growth. You may ask – what about Jim? Well, as I finish this wonderful effort of self-awareness, I am quite comfortable with where I have ended up so far. Yes, I will continue to grow, but will I inch along or will I make giant leaps in spiritual self-awareness? No one knows, and that is the wonderful thing about being human. We all have the opportunity to look forward to what this wonderful life and universe has in store for us. We need to embrace it and be in awe of the magnificence of just being alive and living in this universe we all call home.

So, what about you? You have followed my journey to this point, and I am sure you have formed your thoughts about your spirituality at this point in your life, and I am sure that it might be quite different than mine. As I have said many times before, each and every one of us is on our own journey, and these journeys and the conclusions you draw from it will probably be different for every one of us. That's okay. The important thing is that you take the journey, and that you are satisfied with your spiritual self-awareness at this point in your life.

May peace, love and happiness be with you always. God bless you.

ACKNOWLEDGMENTS

I would like to acknowledge the following people for their editing contributions and guidance.

My wife, Helen M. Russ, for her editing comments and support over the last several years while I was studying, researching, and writing. She is wonderful at keeping me focused in life, and not letting me think too highly of myself.

My daughter, Angelee M. Russ, for her numerous comments and editing that required me to spend many hours contemplating changes and making grammatical corrections. Darn her!

I want to thank my Aunt Carol Johnson and my Uncle Reverend Rollin E. Johnson for reading my document and providing their thoughts and input. I want to particularly thank them for making me realize that our spiritual journeys never end. We will constantly grow, each and every day of our lives. Thank you again.

Lastly, I want to thank all of the experts, professors and authors listed in the bibliography that provided the course material, books, and website information that provided me with the bulk of information to help me on my journey. Additionally, I want to mention that I have also taken quick bits of information at times from the internet which are not listed in the bibliography, but those pieces are just as important even though they may not be referenced. Whether I quoted you directly or used your words in places to better express myself, I am deeply indebted to all of you for your help. Thank you.

BIBLIOGRAPHY

This bibliography is not structured on the strict rules associated with research papers and academic standards. Instead, I loosely listed the sources chronologically as they are encountered in my work, by category.

COURSES

Religions of the Axial Age, a Great Course taught by Professor Mark W. Muesse of Rhodes College. The Axial Age was from 800 – 200 BCE and was one of the most creative and influential eras in world history.

Judaism, a Great Course that was presented by Professor Isaiah M. Gafni of the Hebrew University in Jerusalem.

Christianity, a Great Course that was presented by Professor Luke Timothy Johnson of Emory University. He is a former Benedictine monk and teacher at the Yale Divinity School.

Islam, a Great Course presented by Professor John L. Esposito of Georgetown University. He also serves a vital role as a consultant to the

Department of State, as well as a consultant to corporations and other governments on the subject of Islam.

The Big Questions of Philosophy, a Great Course taught by David Kyle Johnson of King's College in Pennsylvania.

Philosophy of Mind: Brains, Consciousness, and Thinking Machines, a Great Course taught by Patrick Grim B. Phil., Ph.D. of the State University of New York at Stony Brook.

Philosophy of Religion, a Great Course taught by Professor James Hall from the University of Richmond.

The Spiritual Brain: Science and Religious Experience, a Great Course taught by Dr. Andrew Newberg of the Myrna Brind Center of Integrative Medicine at Thomas Jefferson University Hospital. He is board certified in internal and nuclear medicine, but more importantly for us, he has spent a great deal of time studying religious and spiritual experiences and the effects they have on the brain, and vice-versa.

Einstein's Relativity and the Quantum Revolution: Modern Physics for Non-Scientists, 2nd Edition, a Great Course taught by Professor Richard Wolfson of Middlebury College. Professor Wolfson did a very good job of making the course material understandable on such a difficult subject.

The Higgs Boson and Beyond, a Great Course taught by Professor Sean Carroll of the California Institute of Technology.

The Theory of Everything: The Quest to Explain All Reality, a Great Course taught by Professor Don Lincoln of the Fermi National Accelerator Laboratory. He is also a guest speaker on high energy physics at the University of Notre Dame, and he received his PhD in experimental particle physics from Rice University. He was also a member of the team that discovered the top quark in 1995 and a member of the team that confirmed the existence of the Higgs boson in 2012. He has published many books and articles as well as given hundreds of lectures on four continents.

Redefining Reality: The Intellectual Implications of Modern Science, a Great Course taught by Professor Steven Gimbel of Gettysburg College, where he serves as the Chair of the Philosophy Department. He has received various teaching awards, and he has published numerous articles and four books.

BOOKS

The Evolution of God by Robert Wright. Its primary focus is the Abrahamic religions of Judaism, Christianity, and Islam.

Zealot by Reza Aslan, which sheds light on the historical Jesus.

WEBSITES

The following are just the key websites. There are other references in the work to Wikipedia etc., but I feel these are the key ones.

Baha'i faith - Information found on Wikipedia at: https://simple.wikipedia.org/wiki/Bahá%27í_Faith

Atheism and Agnosticism – Information found on Wikipedia at this site: https://simple.wikipedia.org/wiki/Atheism

Paganism – Information found at the following sites:

https://www.learnreligions.com/do-pagans-worship-the-devil-2561845

https://en.wikipedia.org/wiki/Paganism

The Miracle at Sokółka can be found at the following website: vision-sofjesuschrist.com/weeping2124.html

The following website from Las Cumbres Observatory explains the **photoelectric effect:** https://lco.global/spacebook/light/light-particle/

Quantum Entanglement explained at: https://www.cnet.com/news/physicists-prove-einsteins-spooky-quantum-entanglement/

Chaos Theory website at : https://simple.wikipedia.org/wiki/Chaos_theory

The South Africa Truth and Reconciliation Commission to find justice, reconciliation, and forgiveness for the atrocities that occurred during apartheid on Wikipedia at: https://en.wikipedia.org/wiki/Truth_and_Reconciliation_Commission_(South_Africa)

Archbishop Tutu quote from the website: https://law.pepperdine.edu/straus/training-and-conferences/forgiveness-reconciliation-healing.htm

Robert Jastrow information found at his website on Wikipedia at : https://en.wikipedia.org/wiki/Robert_Jastrow

9 781977 236111